THE CATHOLIC UNIVERSITY OF AMERICA
CANON LAW STUDIES
NO. 95

THE PROPER BISHOP FOR ORDINATION AND DIMISSORIAL LETTERS

AN HISTORICAL SYNOPSIS AND COMMENTARY

A DISSERTATION

SUBMITTED TO THE FACULTY OF CANON LAW OF THE CATHOLIC UNIVERSITY OF AMERICA IN PARTIAL FULFILLMENT OF THE REQUIREMENTS FOR THE DEGREE OF DOCTOR OF CANON LAW

BY

JOHN M. MOEDER, J.C.L.
PRIEST OF THE DIOCESE OF WICHITA, KANSAS

THE CATHOLIC UNIVERSITY OF AMERICA
WASHINGTON, D. C.
1935

Nihil Obstat

VALENTINUS T. SCHAAF, O.F.M., J.C.D.
Censor Deputatus

Washingtonii, D.C., die 14 Maii 1935

Imprimatur

✠ AUGUSTINUS JOANNES, D.D.
Episcopus Wichitensis

Wichitensis, die 17 Maii 1935

Printed by THE DOLPHIN PRESS *Philadelphia, Pa.*

To

Laurence E. Keefe

in heartfelt appreciation this study is
sincerely and gratefully
dedicated

TABLE OF CONTENTS

PART TWO

Commentary

CHAPTER ONE

Proper Bishop of Ordination

CHAPTER TWO

Dimissorial Letters

CHAPTER THREE

Proper Bishop for the Ordination of Religious

FOREWORD

THE first part of this study is an historical conspectus of the title of ordination, the proper bishop of ordination and dimissorial letters. It is an attempt to give an historical setting to the second part of this dissertation.

A commentary on canons 955-967 of the Code of Canon Law makes up the content of the second part. Canons 956 and 964 receive special attention because of their particular importance and because of the canonical difficulties connected with them. Accordingly chapter one of the commentary treats of canon 956, the ordination of the diocesan clergy. The second chapter is a discussion of the canonical norms of the New Code with regard to dimissorial letters. Ordination of religious (canon 964) is the subject matter of the final chapter of the commentary.

The writer expresses his heartfelt thanks to all those who assisted him in this work. To those who helped him more than they might realize with their generosity and kind encouragement the writer is sincerely grateful. He expresses his appreciation to his Bishop, the Most Rev. Aug. J. Schwertner, D.D., to the Faculty of the Graduate School of Canon Law, the Reverend Doctors Schaaf, Motry, Roelker, Lardone, and Mr. Fox. He wishes to thank, likewise, the librarians of the Catholic University for their assistance which they rendered on many occasions.

PART ONE

HISTORICAL SYNOPSIS

CHAPTER ONE

Title of Ordination

An historical conspectus of this study must necessarily include a brief sketch of the title of ordination. The concept of the ordination title in the early centuries of the Church was identified closely with the proper bishop for ordination. Out of the regulations concerning the *titulus ordinationis* came the dimissorial letters.

The word *titulus,* as used in ecclesiastical terminology,[1] originated in Rome.[2] It designated churches at which clerics were stationed in order to distinguish these churches from the other ecclesiastical institutions of Rome which gave clerics no definite and lasting residence. Since the third century a parish had its own buildings set aside for divine worship. Before these buildings were devoted to sacred use they had been in the possession of private owners who donated them to the parish. The name of the owner or builder of the larger private Roman dwellings was inscribed above the entrance. This inscription was called *titulus* which was here taken in the common, original sense of the word. It designated the house, serving very much the same purpose of house numbers on a modern street. It also indicated to whom the right of possession belonged. When dwellings became the property of a parish they generally retained the name of their former owner. Because of this it was common to meet such expressions, as *titulus Julii Pudentis, titulus Caeciliae.* Thus the word *titulus* received the meaning of possession and ownership of houses.

1 "Titulus, ἐπιγραφή, χαρακτήρ, inscriptio, nota, index, elogium quo res dignoscitur, et quid valeat, contineat, cuius sit, cur facta sit, monstratur, ut titulus sepulcri, aedium, libri, statuae, picturae, et huiusmodi. 'Titus' praenomine R. quod a τιτός, honoratus a τίω: quia honor et pretium suum rebus a titulo accedit."—Forcellini, *Lexicon Totius Latinitatis,* Editio in Germania Prima, Schneebergae, 1835, T. IV, p. 326.

2 Fuchs, Vincent, *Der Ordinationstitel von seiner Entstehung bis auf Innocenz III,* Bonn, 1930, p. 7 ff.

As the number of the faithful increased so grew the need of more priests and of more members of the lower clergy at various churches in the city of Rome. It became necessary that the clergy be definitely and permanently appointed. There were then no seminaries as they exist today. Each individual church took care of its clergy. The cleric was ascribed permanently to one church and he was ordained for the perpetual service of that church.

Perpetual ascription to a title or to a certain church to which the cleric (*intitulatus*) devoted his ministry constituted the title of ordination in the early ecclesiastical forum. The church of the cleric's title gave him an income.[3] In virtue of this the ordination title signified principally and primarily the office or post which demanded the service of the cleric. The remuneration or sustenance of the cleric was only secondary. The cleric, because of his title, had a definite assignment in the ministry and also his proper support.[4] He could not leave the church for which he was ordained without the consent of the bishop.[5] He was known as *titulatus* or *intitulatus*.[6] No one was to be ordained without a certain title.

Innocent I, writing to Bishop Decentius Eugubinus in 402 calls the churches of Rome *tituli*. "De fermento vero, quod die dominica, per *titulos* mittimus. . . ."[7] Likewise the *Liber Pontificalis* makes mention of the *tituli*.[8] A recent author refers to the *Liber Pontificalis* as a source with regard to the *tituli* of Rome.[9]

The word "title" soon took on a broader meaning. It began to designate not only the church but also the ecclesias-

[3] F. X. Wernz, *Jus Decretalium, Romae*, 1906, II, n. 90.

[4] Thomassinus, L., *Vetus et Nova Ecclesiae Disciplina*, Parisiis, 1688, P. II, Lib. I, cap. 9, n. 2.

[5] Fuchs, *Ordinationstitel*, p. 90 ff; Thomassinus, *Vetus et Nova Ecclesiae Disciplina*, P. II, Lib. I, cap. 10, n. 1-2; cap. 2, n. 7.

[6] Paul Hinschius, *System des Katholischen Kirchenrechts*, Berlin, 1869, I, 63.

[7] Mansi 3, 1028.

[8] L. Duchesne, *Liber Pontificalis*, Paris, 1886, I, 126.

[9] Guiseppe Buonocore, *Il "Titulus Canonicus"*, Napoli, 1933, p. 111.

tical office of the clergy.[10] No cleric, however, as stated above, could abandon his title without the bishop's permission. Hefele [11] calls this prohibition a very old regulation. It is met with in the Canons of the Apostles.[12] The First Council of Arles, 314 [13] made express mention of the law. A clear statement of this norm is found in the Council of Nice, 325 [14] and in the Council of Chalcedon, 451.[15]

Authors call attention to the fact that at an early date, i. e. between the Councils of Nice, 325 and the Council of Chalcedon, 451 exceptions were made to the rule.[16] These exceptions were in the form of absolute ordinations. In 379 St. Jerome was ordained without any title by Paulinus.[17] Likewise the monk Macedonius was ordained without attachment to any church by Flavian, Bishop of Antioch (381-404).[18]

[10] Hinschius, *System des Kath. Kirchenrechts*, I, 63.

[11] Carl Joseph von Hefele, *Conciliengeschichte*, Freiburg im Breisgau, 2 ed., 1873, I, 804, n. 1.

[12] Canon 14: "Si quis presbyter, vel diaconus, vel omnino ex clericorum catalogo, relicta sua parochia, in aliam abscesserit, et cum penitus transierit, praeter sui episcopi sententiam in alia parochia maneat, eum non amplius celebrare jubemus."—Mansi 1, 31; Hefele 1, 804-805.

[13] Canon 2: "De his qui in quibuscumque locis ordinati fuerint ministri, in ipsis locis perseverent."—Mansi 2, 471; Hefele 1, 205. Also canon 21, —Mansi 2, 473; Hefele 1, 216.

[14] Canon 15: "Propter multum tumultum et seditiones quae fiunt, omnino visum est ut consuetudo, quae praeter canonem in nonnullis partibus invenitur, tollatur: ut a civitate in civitatem nec episcopus, nec presbyter, nec diaconus transeat. Si quis autem post sanctae et magnae synodi definitionem tale quidpiam aggressus fuerit...ecclesiae restituetur, cui episcopus vel presbyter ordinatus fuerit."—Mansi 2, 674; c. 19, C. VII, q. 1; Hefele 1, 419.

[15] Canon 10: "Non licere clerico in duarum civitatum ecclesiis eodem tempore in catalogum referri, et in ea qua a principio ordinatus est, et in ea, in quam, tamquam majorem, confugit, propter inanis gloriae cupiditatem: eos autem qui hoc faciunt, propriae ecclesiae restitui, in qua ab initio ordinati sunt, ut illic solum ministrent..."—Mansi 7, 362; Hefele 2, 510; Harduin 2, 606.

[16] S. Many, *Praelectiones de Sacra Ordinatione*, Parisiis, 1905, n. 130; Fuchs, *Ordinationstitel*, pp. 103-111.

[17] *Liber Contra Joannem Hierosolymitanum*, S. Eusebii Hieronymi, n. 41, —MPL 23, 393.

[18] *Religiosa Historia*, Theodoret, n. 13,—MPG 82, 1402.

The classical example of early absolute ordinations is the ordination of Paulinus, later the holy Bishop of Nola, at Barcelona 394 or 395. While on his way to Nola where he wished to lead the life of an ascetic near the grave of St. Felix he spent some time in Barcelona. The people sought him out in order to have him ordained a priest. He would not listen to their pleadings because he wanted to go to Nola. Finally he placed the condition that he be not ascribed to any church. Upon this condition he was ordained.[19] Absolute ordinations will receive further consideration later on in this chapter.

The history of the title of ordination is the history of the relationship between ordination and assignment of the cleric to a definite church.[20] In the early centuries of the Church the two were identified, so much so that when they were separated by absolute ordinations and by the title of patrimony the question arose whether the reception of Orders was valid. Authors [21] are generally in agreement that the expression *ordi-*

[19] *Epistola* I, Sti. Paulini Nolani Episcopi, n. 10,—MPL 61, 159.

[20] Fuchs, *Ordinationstitel*, p. 11.

[21] Wernz, *Jus Decretalium*, II, n. 91, note 31; Hinschius, *System des Kathol. Kirchenrechts*, I, p. 77, n. 5; Thomassinus, *Vetus et Nova Ecclesiae Disciplina*, P. II, Lib. I, cap. 9, n. 1: "In Concilio Placentino anno 1095 irrita pronuntiata est ordinatio quae sine titulo fieret. Ea irritatio non spectabat nisi ad Ordinum executionem."—The Canon 15 of the Council of Piacenza reads: "Decernimus, ut sine titulo facta ordinatio irrita habeatur, et in qua quislibet titulatus est in ea perpetuo perseveret. Omnino autem in duabus aliquem titulari non liceat, sed unusquisque in qua titulatus est in ea tantum canonicus."—Mansi 20, 806; Hefele 5, 218; c. 2, D. LXX; Harduin 6B, 1715.

It is necessary also to quote here Canon 6 of the Council of Chalcedon, 451: "Nullum absolute ordinari debere presbyterum aut diaconum, nec quemlibet in gradu ecclesiastico, nisi specialiter ecclesiae civitatis, aut possessionis, aut martyrii, aut monasterii, qui ordinandus est pronuntietur. Qui vero absolute ordinantur, decrevit Sancta Synodus irritam haberi huiusmodi manus impositionem, et nunquam posse ministrare, ad ordinantis injuriam." —Mansi 7, 362; Hefele 2, 510; Harduin 2, 603; c. 1, D. LXX. Van Espen commenting on this canon says that it is the opinion of canonists and theologians that this canon "similesque canones, invaliditatem Ordinationis praeferentes, interpretantur de nullitate non absoluta, sed tantum *quoad executionem*, id est, quod Ordinatus nequeat licite exequi seu obire functiones Ordinis suscepti; quamvis *valide* sit ordinatus, ideoque si functiones illicite et contra Canones obiret, equidem exerceret valide."—*Jus Ecclesiasticum*, Venetiis, 1769, P. II, Sect. I, Tit. IX, *De Sacramento Ordinis*, n. 12.

natio irrita found in the canons with regard to absolute ordinations meant that the one ordained was suspended from the exercise of the Orders received. His ordination was valid.[22]

After the Council of Chalcedon, 451, the law of permanent ascription to a particular church was retained intact up to the twelfth century. The title of ordination was not done away with at this time but it received a different signification. Before this change came in the twelfth century many councils made regulations keeping alive the original concept of the ordination title. A great number of abuses, however, had crept in as the statutes of the councils and synods indicate.

A summary reference to the canons and statutes of the councils and synods held after the year 451 (Council of Chalcedon) and before the year 1179 (Third Council of the Lateran) will help to clarify what has been said thus far.

The subscriptions to the first synod of Rome, 499, under Pope Simmachus give an interesting testimony of the concept of the ordination title at the time. For example, " Valens, presbyter, tituli Sanctae Sabinae subscripsi ", or " Paulinus, presbyter, tituli Julii subscripsi." [23]

The Council of Valencia, 524, clearly stressed the necessity of a title of ordination.[24] Absolute ordinations, i. e. without any title were positively forbidden by the Councils of Aachen, 789,[25] Frankfurt, 794,[26] Rome, 826,[27] Meaux, 845,[28] London, 1125,[29] and Avranche, 1172.[30]

22 Fuchs, *Ordinationstitel*, p. 11.

23 Mansi 8, 235; Hefele 2, 625; Harduin 2, 961-962.

24 Caput 6: "... Sed nec illum sanctorum sacerdotum quispiam ordinet, qui localem se futurum primitus non spoponderit: ut per hoc nullus a regula vel disciplina ecclesiastica deviare permittatur impune." — Mansi 8, 622; Harduin 2, 1070; Hefele 2, 710.

25 Mansi 17B, 223; Hefele 3, 666; Harduin 4, 833.

26 Mansi 17B, 267; Hefele 3, 691; Harduin 4, 907.

27 Mansi 14, 1004; Hefele 4, 48.

28 Mansi 14, 831; Hefele 4, 117; Harduin 4, 1492.

29 Mansi 21, 331; Hefele 5, 391; Harduin 6B, 1126.

30 Mansi 22, 140; Hefele 5, 686; Harduin 6B, 1634.

The clarity and precision which marked the laws of the early councils leave no doubt as to the legislation of the Church on the ordination title in the first thousand years of her existence. Further discussion will show that the laws remained equally clear in later centuries.

Clerics were not to be ordained without a title.[31] They were to remain perpetually ascribed to their church [32] and even if they left they were to be returned to their former church.[33] The Council of Melfi, 1089, in canon 9 forbade the existence of *acephali* who were keeping themselves in the palaces of the great.[34]

The legislative enactments of the Councils, which have been reviewed, accentuated that canon 6 of the Council of Chalcedon, 451, was the nucleus of the law. This law in the Church made an ordination title necessary. As stated above this primarily meant ascription to a certain church. The support of the cleric was of secondary importance. In reading the Councils one cannot fail to notice that in practice the law was neglected. At first the infractions were few. Prior to the fourth century no absolute ordinations are in evidence.[35] In the fourth century the anchorites, cenobites and ascetics brought about ordinations without a title, at least to some extent. A few years after the Council of Chalcedon, 451, Bishop Rusticus of Narbonne wrote to Pope Leo the Great with regard to the uncanonical ordinations in Provence. Pope Leo answered in the year 458 or 459. He called the ordinations in his official decision a *vana creatio*.[36] The Gallic Synods of this time men-

[31] Council of Clermont (1095), Canon 13: "...ut omnes clericus ad eum titulum, ad quem primum ordinatus est, semper ordinetur."—Mansi 20, 817; Harduin 6B, 1719; Hefele 5, 223.

[32] Third Council of Tours, 813, canon 14.—Mansi 14, 85; Harduin 4, 1025.

[33] Canon 3 of the Council of Seville, 619.—Mansi 10, 557-558; Harduin 3, 558; Hefele 3, 72.

[34] Mansi 20, 723; Harduin 6B, 1686; Hefele 5, 195.

[35] Fuchs, *Ordinationstitel*, p. 103, note 2.

[36] Fuchs, *Ordinationstitel*, p. 130; *Epistola* CLXVII, Leonis Magni, n. 1. —MPL. 54, 1203.

tioned uncanonical ordinations which took place even before the Council of Chalcedon.[37]

Despite the prohibitions, particularly of canon 6 of the Council of Chalcedon, the number of ordinations without title grew steadily.[38] This non-observance of the law rests on the fact that in time the growth of the Church not only increased the number of ecclesiastical offices but also united to these offices certain temporal possessions. Title began to mean benefice.[39] In consequence of the reorganization of church property the number of titles was not sufficient and bishops ordained without title. At the end of the eleventh century these ordinations had grown more common. A large number of *clerici vagrantes* or *acephali* appeared. The Third Council of the Lateran, 1179,[40] set out to correct the abuses. In that Council Pope Alexander III made the law which brought about a marked change in the prevailing discipline of the earlier centuries. The change was effected by accident. Pope Alexander had not intended to introduce a different concept of the ordination title. He was intent rather upon restraining the bishops from ordaining clerics without titles. He, therefore, demanded that bishops support any deacon or priest whom they ordained without title. Bishops were commanded to care for a cleric so ordained until he was given a title unless he had a sufficient patrimony to support himself.[41] The law, however, was misunderstood. The common interpretation given to it was that the sole title of ordination was no longer permanent service at

[37] Canon 8 of the First Council of Orange, 441.—Mansi 6, 437; Hefele 2, 293; Second Council of Arles, 452 (the date of this Council is sometimes given as 443).—Mansi 7, 880; Hefele 2, 300.

[38] Hinschius, *System des Kathol. Kirchenrechts*, I, pp. 63-64.

[39] C. 3, X, *de clericis conjugatis*, III, 3.

[40] Cap. 5, Mansi 22, 220; Hefele 5, 712-713; Harduin 6B, 1676; c. 4, X, *de praebendis et dignitatibus*, III, 5.

[41] "Episcopus, si aliquem sine certo titulo, de quo necessaria vitae percipiat, in diaconum vel presbyterum ordinaverit, tamdiu necessaria ei ministret, donec in aliqua ei ecclesia convenientia stipendia militiae clericalis assignet: nisi forte talis qui ordinatur, extiterit, qui de sua vel paterna haereditate subsidium vitae possit habere."—C. 4, X, *de praebendis et dignitatibus*, III, 5; Mansi 22, 220; Harduin 6B, 1676; Hefele 5, 712-713.

a certain church. Canonists considered that the possession of sufficient income for the support of a cleric was henceforth the primary requisite for the ordination title. It was not to matter whether the cleric received an honest sustenance from the church or from his private property or from paternal inheritance.

Alexander III had thought to put an end to the ordinations without title. He succeeded as to deacons and priests but the law did not include ordinations to minor Orders. Innocent III in 1198 extended the requirement of a title to the subdiaconate.[42] A further extension of an ordination title to minor Orders by means of papal mandate met the opposition of the bishops and did not become effective. The Glossa [43] and Panormitanus [44] required a title for minor Orders but the majority of contemporary canonists did not hesitate to adopt the opposite opinion. They agreed with Stephan, Bishop of Tournay (1135-1203) who, when urged by Pope Celestine III, or Innocent III, to express his views on this subject said: "With all respect to your Holiness, Holy Father, to exact a title for minor Orders seem to me to be a new and unusual custom. Hitherto the most reliable canons have, in the exaction of titles, confined themselves to the priesthood and diaconate, at least, so had it been decreed by the Council of Lateran held under Pope Alexander of happy memory. Many of us assisted at that Council and approved the decision unanimously passed, but then it only had reference to priests and deacons. We heartily accept this law, we approve of it unreservedly and with the grace of God we will observe it as faithfully in the future as we have done in the past. Moreover, it is equally impossible for us to remember all those on whom we have conferred minor Orders or deaconship and to give them benefices for their sustenance. Better by far to renounce ordaining than to impose upon one's self such weighty responsibilities." [45]

[42] C. 16, X, *de praebendis et dignitatibus*, III, 5.

[43] C. 1, D. LXX.

[44] C. 2, n. 2, X, *de praebendis et dignitatibus*, III, 5.

[45] Stephanus Tornacensis ep. 194 ad Papam,—Migne, P. L. 211, 477, (translation taken from Peries, "Titulus Ordinationis", *A. E. R.*, 13 (1895), 274.

The fundamental idea of the legislation enacted by Alexander III was not exactly new.[46] It was his opinion that the cleric should receive his support from the church to which he had been ascribed. He determined that the old Apostolic principle be carried out in practice.[47] His law was an act of solicitude for the clergy. He did not intend to change the title of ordination. Nevertheless, this law marked a departure from the old concept. Innocent III completed the change when hardly three decades later, in 1208, he recognized the new title of ordination. It was incorporated into the common law of the Church in the Decretals of Gregory IX.[48] The word title no longer meant solely ascription to a certain church. It began to mean a guarantee of clerical support.[49] The acceptation of the ordination title under this new meaning was declared at the Council of Beziers, 1233.[50]

The laws of the Church from the beginning of the thirteenth century no longer mentioned the perpetual ascription of a cleric to a particular church as a requirement for ordination. The Councils, instead, insisted upon an ecclesiastical benefice or patrimony as a requisite for ordination.[51]

[46] Fuchs, *Ordinationstitel*, p. 269.

[47] Innocent III in 1210 referred to the Apostolic practice: " Cum secundum Apostolum, qui altario servit, vivere debeat de altari: et qui ad onus eligitur, repelli non debeat a mercede: patet a simili, ut Clerici vivere debeant de patrimonio Jesu Christi, cuius obsequio deputantur: ut ipsa nominis ratio persuadet."—C. 16, X, *de praebendis et dignitatibus*, III, 5.

[48] C. 23, X, *de praebendis et dignitatibus*, III, 5.

[49] Fuchs, *Ordinationstitel*, p. 277.

[50] Canon 6: "....et sine titulo patrimoniali centum solidorum Turonensium ad minus ecclesiastico beneficio competenti, sicut in jure canonico cautum est, ordinandus de cetero nullatenus admittatur."—Mansi 23, 271; Harduin 7, 209.

[51] Canon 3 of a Council of an uncertain location in Spain after 1215: " Praecipimus ne quis promoveatur in subdiaconum, diaconum, vel presbyterum, nisi habeat competens secundum qualitatem terrae beneficium ecclesiasticum, vel saltem sufficiens patrimonium, ad cuius quasi titulum ordinatur."—Mansi 22, 1090. Canon 26 of the Council of Beziers, 1246: " Ut presbyteris idonea et sufficiens portio assignetur in ecclesiis."—Mansi 23, 697; Harduin 7, 411; Hefele 5, 1143. Likewise canon 9 of the Council of Narbonne, 1228.—Mansi 23, 23; Harduin 7, 147; Hefele 5, 943; canon 32

The creation of the title of patrimony for ordination brought to light more clearly the existence of another title, i. e. the *titulus beneficii,* which in essence dates from the sixth century.[52] Many [53] says that at the end of the fifth century the temporal possessions of the Church were divided into as many parts as there were clerics to be supported. The Church perfected the division at the close of the ninth century. Each individual portion of temporal goods was entirely separate from the other, so that, when a cleric died his portion of sustenance did not revert to the common treasury or property as before, but it was said to be vacant. These portions, completely separate, were called *beneficia* or *praebendae.* Since clerics were to be ordained *ad titulum* or to a certain church, they were by that very fact also assigned to the *beneficia* or *praebendae* for their food and sustenance. As a direct consequence of this the *beneficium* or *praebenda* was called *titulus* and the *titulus* was called *beneficium.* This assimilation or identification of title and benefice found clear expression in the Council of Clermont, 1095.[54]

of the Fourth Council of Lateran, 1215: "...portio presbyteris ipsis sufficiens assignetur."—Mansi 22, 1019; Harduin 7, 43; Hefele 5, 892. Caput 8 of the Synod of Exeter, 1287.—Mansi 24, 796E; Harduin 7, 1084D. Council of Prague, 1346, cap. De aetate et qualitate ad sacros ordines: "...utrum habeat perpetuum beneficium ecclesiasticum vel sufficiens patrimonium volens ad sacros ordines promoveri."—Mansi 26, 78C. Council of Lyons, 1449, cap. 13: "Praelati neminem promoveant ad sacros ordines nisi quem constabit obtinere beneficium ecclesiasticum vel actualiter habere patrimonium." —Mansi 32, 96. Council of Mainz, 1549, cap. 81: "Nec quisquam ordinandus recipiatur nisi ad certum titulum ecclesiastici beneficii, quod sit perpetuum, a quo non possit ad inordinatum alicuius placitum promoveri, aut cui de proprio patrimonio sufficienter sit provisum."—Mansi 35B, 1555-1556. Provincial Council of Narbonne, 1551, canon 8: "Itaque nemo sacros ordines consequatur cui speciatim destinata ad victum bona non sint; sive a sacerdotio, seu beneficio aliquo sive a patrimonio petantur."—Mansi 33, 1254. Council of Avignon, 1455, canon 17.—Mansi 32, 188. Council of Rouen, 1445, canon 16: "Item quod ipsi sic promovendi habeant beneficium seu patrimonium vel titulum verum a suis parentibus et propinquis sine fraude."—Mansi 32, 28.

[52] Wernz, *Jus Decretalium,* II, n. 91.

[53] Many, *De Sacra Ordinatione,* n. 134.

[54] Canon 12: "Ut nulli clericorum liceat deinceps in duabus civitatibus duas *praebendas* obtinere, cum duos *titulos* non possit habere."—Mansi 20, 817; c. 30, X, *de iure patronatus,* III, 38.

The Third Council of the Lateran, 1179, did not originate a new title, i. e. the *titulus beneficii*. It but gave the title of benefice a further development which in nucleus was contained in the legislation of the Council of Chalcedon [55] and which since the sixth century gradually grew into the jurisprudence of the Church.

Canon 6 of the Council of Chalcedon likewise gave origin to the *titulus professionis religiosae.*[56] This title was the title of ordination for the monks. As monasticism developed and spread the regulations concerning the ordination title were gradually applied to the monks.[57] The solemn religious profession of the monk was his title for ordination because it assured him of sustenance. He was attached to religion by an indissoluble bond and could not obtain his support elsewhere.[58]

There existed then in the first years of the thirteenth century three ordination titles, i. e. title of benefice, title of patrimony and title of religious profession. The title of benefice and the title of religious profession (*titulus monasterii also known as the titulus paupertatis*) had found their origin in the early centuries of the Church. The Council of Chalcedon had given them a definite place in ecclesiastical legislation.[59]

The Third Council of the Lateran, 1179, had given rise to the third title, the title of patrimony. " . . . si habeat ex sua vel paterna hereditate subsidium vitae: sed tantum in hoc casu episcopum, qui eum sine beneficio sacris initiavit, non teneri eidem necessaria vitae sub-ministrare." [60] Wernz [61] defines the

[55] Wernz, *Jus Decretalium*, II, n. 91.

[56] Wernz, *Jus Decretalium*, II, n. 91.

[57] Hinschius, *System des Kathol. Kirchenrechts*, I, p. 65.

[58] Many, *De Sacra Ordinatione*, n. 134.

[59] The ordinary title for the regular clergy was the *titulus monasterii sive religionis sive professionis religiosae.*—C. 1, D. LXX; Wernz, *Jus Decretalium*, II, n. 92; Gasparri, *De Sacra Ordinatione*, n. 856; Many, *De Sacra Ordinatione*, n. 134. Hinschius remarks that the regulations concerning the ordination title had no direct application to the monks. Later on when in the act of ordination a title was required the religious profession of the monk served as a title because it assured the monk of sustenance.—*System des Kathol. Kirchenrechts*, 65.

[60] Mansi 22, 220.

[61] *Jus Decretalium*, II, n. 92.

title of patrimony as follows: "Et *titulus* quidem *patrimonii* sunt bona propria ipsius clerici ordinandi *legitime* acquisita, *sufficientia* ad congruam sustentationem iuxta taxam synodalem vel probatam regionis consuetudinem, *certa immobilia* vel saltem ita *secura,* ut immobilibus aequiparentur." This title led to many abuses in virtue of the interpretation given to the text of the Third Council of the Lateran.[62] The clerics ordained with the title of patrimony did not consider themselves bound to serve any church because they took care of themselves. The rich were easily ordained. They enjoyed the clerical privileges and shouldered few of its burdens with the result that there was a great number of idle and unnecessary clerics.

The Fathers of the Council of Trent sought to remedy the abuses. " . . . Patrimonium vero vel pensionem obtinentes ordinari posthac non possint, nisi illi, quos episcopus iudicaverit assumendos pro necessitate vel commoditate ecclesiarum suarum; eo quoque prius perspecto, patrimonium illud vel pensionem vere ab eis obtineri, taliaque esse, quae eis ad vitam sustentandam satis sint."[63] " . . . Quum nullus debeat ordinari, qui iudicio sui episcopi non sit utilis aut necessarius suis ecclesiis, sancta synodus, vestigiis sexti canonis concilii Chalcedonensis inhaerendo, statuit, ut nullus in posterum ordinetur, qui illi ecclesiae aut pio loco, pro cuius necessitate aut utilitate assumitur, non adscribatur, ubi suis fungatur muneribus, nec incertis vagetur sedibus."[64] The Council of Trent did not remove the title of patrimony. It tried in some way to return to the old legislation of ascription. The cleric regardless of his order or of his title of ordination was to remain at the church for whose needs and usefulness he had been ordained. This church he was bound to serve by exercising the functions of his order.

At the Tridentine Council another title came into existence. It was the title of pension which Wernz defines thus: "Titulus

[62] Wernz, *Jus Decretalium,* II, n. 91.

[63] Sess. XXI, *de reformatione,* cap. 2.

[64] Sess. XXIII, *de reformatione,* cap. 16.

vero pensionis est census quidam aut fructibus beneficii ecclesiastici vel aliis bonis ecclesiasticis impositus aut per ecclesiasticam vel laicam personam singularem vel communitatem praestandus, sed super bonis immobilibus vel aliis bonis iisdem quoad securitatem aequiparatis v. g. obligationibus Status fundatus sit oportet." [65] The requirements of the title of pension, almost without exception, were the same as those of the title of patrimony. "The only real difference between the two was the nature of the property or fund which insured to the cleric his income. In the case of the *pensio* the revenues were derived from an endowment. . . . The *pensio* was obtained either from church property, or from possessions which originally belonged to lay persons. This gave rise to the distinction commonly found among authors between the *pensio ecclesiastica* and the *pensio laica*. When the *pensio ecclesiastica* was made up of the revenues of a diocese, and perpetually established by its bishop, it became a real *titulus beneficii*. The *pensio laica* was simply reckoned as a patrimony, and it was the duty of the bishop to determine, according to the custom of the place, what amount of annual income was necessary for the founding of a title, in case some lay person desired to establish such." [66]

Schmalzgrueber [67] in his reply to the query whether the *titulus pensionis* was a sufficient title for ordination answers in the affirmative: "Sumitur ex trid. sess. 21, cap. 2. de reform. ubi eodem modo de patrimonio, quo de pensione loquitur, quod scilicet ordinari ad utramque clericus possit; si ita necessitas, vel commoditas ecclesiarum exegerit." Schmalzgrueber indicates that the title of pension can be reduced to the title of patrimony.

A further study of the ordination title reveals that the discipline with regard to it followed the change of the term which came in the twelfth century. It perdured from the Council of

[65] Wernz, *Jus Decretalium*, II, n. 92.

[66] Peries, "Titulus Ordinationis", *A. E. R.*, 13 (1895), 351.

[67] F. Schmalzgrueber, *Jus Ecclesiasticum Universum*, Lib. I, Tit. XI, n. 57.

Trent to the Council of the Vatican. Provincial Councils during this time insistently demanded a sufficient title for ordination whether that be title of benefice, of pension or of patrimony.[68]

The command that a cleric be not ordained unless useful for some church or unless perpetually ascribed to it is also found in the Councils from the middle of the sixteenth century onward.[69]

[68] Provincial Synod of Ravenna, 1568, cap. 5, De Ordine: "Animadvertent etiam episcopi, ne sacris ordinibus aliquem initient, qui vere ecclesiasticum beneficium, pensionem, vel patrimonium eius victui sufficiens, iuxta eiusdem concilii decretum, non obtineat."—Mansi 35A, 622. Synodal Statutes of the diocese of Besancon, 1571, stat. De examine ordinandorum, n. 8: "Promovendi ad ordinem subdiaconatus primo exhibeant titulum beneficii aut pensionis, vel patrimonii sufficientis cuius copiam relinquent penes sigilliferum curiae."—Mansi 36B, 63. Council of Petrokow in the province of Gnesen, 1577, synodal constitutions, lib. I, tit. De temporibus ordinationum: Before any one is ordained inquiry must be made "utrum habeat perpetuum beneficium ecclesiasticum, vel sufficiens patrimonium aut sufficientem provisionem volens ad sacros ordines promoveri."—Mansi 36B, 675. Provincial Council of Toledo, 1582, Actio Tertia, Decr. 31.—Mansi 36B, 176; likewise Decr. 32 of the same Council.—Mansi 36B, 176-177. Provincial Council of Bordeaux, 1583, tit. 14: "Et ne clerici, qui divino ministerio adscripti sunt, cum ordinis sui dedecore mendicare aut sordidum quippiam exercere cogantur, nullus deinceps, iuxta SS. patrum decreta (Trent) ad sacrum subdiaconatus ordinem recipiatur nisi prius legitime constet beneficium ecclesiasticum quod sibi ad victum honeste sufficiat.... Ad patrimonii vero, vel pensionis titulum nullus admittatur, qui non sit utilis, aut necessarius alicui ecclesiae aut pio loco."—Mansi 34A, 760. Council of Mexico, 1585, lib. I, tit. IV, De titulo beneficii, aut patrimonii.—Mansi 34B, 1035. Provincial Council of Avignon, 1594, tit. 19: "Quicumque alicui maiorum ordinem adscribendus est, haec testata faciat, scilicet se aetatis esse legitimae, beneficium sufficiens, vel patrimonium quoties pro necessitate vel utilitate ecclesiae promovebitur, pacifice possidere."—Mansi 34B, 1341D. Provincial Council of Aquileja, 1596, rubric XL: "Idcirco sacri concilii Tridentini decreto inhaerentes statuimus, accurate observandum, ut nemo ad ordinem subdiaconatus admittatur nisi legitime constet, eum ecclesiasticum beneficium, quod sibi ad victum honeste sufficiat, pacifice possidere: ad titulum patrimonii vel pensionis."—Mansi 34B, 1401C. Provincial Council of Naples, 1699, constitutiones, tit. III, cap. VII, n. 4-5.—Mansi 36Ter, 749.

[69] Provincial Council of Rheims, 1564, stat. 12: "Ut omnes clerici sunt certae alicui ecclesiae addicti."—Mansi 33, 1296. Provincial Council of Genoa (before 1574), decreta, cap. XII, n. 3.—Mansi 36B, 577. Provincial

The canons of the Council quoted above show that the early discipline of permanent ascription to a particular church still lingered on in the general law of the church until the Vatican Council. The laws, however, were not faithfully observed everywhere. In some parts the ascription was widely interpreted to mean ascription to a diocese and not to a definite church.[70] This was gradually acclaimed as the custom of the diocese.[71] In virtue of this custom incardination to an entire diocese instead of to an individual church of a diocese was introduced. This has received a place in the Code of Canon Law.[72]

This brief and summary review of the title of ordination will serve as a historical setting to the early and later concept of the proper bishop for ordination and of dimissorial letters. There is no need of a further exposition of the development of the ordination title as far as this study is concerned. It suffiices to have prefaced the study with the early concept of the various titles. The definitions of the titles do not vary in

Council of Rouen, 1581, cap. De episcoporum officiis, n. 6.—Mansi 34A, 633. Second Council of Ravenna, 1582, tit. De sacramento ordinis, n. 10: "Clerici omnes, cum ad aliquem ordinem promoventur per episcopum certae ascribantur ecclesiae, in qua suorum ordinum functiones obeant, illosque in ea tali pietate praestant, ut digni habeantur, qui ad altiorem gradum ascendant, nec ulterius promoveantur, nisi legitime episcopo fidem fecerint se in ecclesia cui adscripti sunt pie ac diligenter praestitisse impositas sibi functiones aut per eos non stetisse quin eas praestiterint."—Mansi 36B, 842. Provincial Council of Cambrai, 1586, tit. X, n. 6.—Mansi 34B, 1239. Provincial Council of Avignon, 1594, tit. 19: "Nemo ad titulum patrimonii ordinetur qui revera patrimonium ad congruam sustentationem sufficiens non habuerit quique alicui ecclesiae non adscribatur quod episcopi observent."—Mansi 34B, 1341B. Provincial Council of Bordeaux, 1624, cap. VI, n. 6.—Mansi 34B, 1558-1559. Innocent XIII, const. "Apostolici Ministerii", May 23, 1723, n. 3, *Fontes*, n. 280; approved by Benedict XIII, const. "In Supremo", Sept. 23, 1724, n. 28, *Fontes*, n. 283. Council of Rome, 1725, tit. VII, cap. 2.—Mansi 34B, 1862. Provincial Council of Mt. Lebanon, 1736, p. II, cap. 14, n. 12.—Mansi 38, 132.

[70] Summary of responses given by the bishops concerning more serious matters of ecclesiastical discipline to be treated in the Vatican Council, Question IX, n. 229-245.—Mansi 49, 349-357.

[71] *Ibidem*, n. 232.—Mansi 49, 350; n. 240.—Mansi 49, 352; n. 241.—Mansi 49, 352.

[72] Canon 111.

later legislation even though their importance and place in the law underwent changes.

There remain a few subsidiary or extraordinary titles of ordination which will be defined briefly.

1. TITULUS MISSIONIS

The *titulus missionis* was unknown at the Tridentine Council.[73] Its introduction into ecclesiastical legislation came with the foundation of the Roman Institutes for the missions at the close of the sixteenth century. On April 22, 1579 the Collegium Anglicanum was erected.[74] In the Bull of erection Gregory XIII [75] granted to the English College at Rome a series of privileges suited to the particular conditions of its students: " Eisdem alumnis, ut, de licentia protectoris ac dicti collegii rectoris consensu, et examine praecedente . . . etiam absque suorum Ordinariorum literis dimissorialibus, *ac sine aliquo beneficii vel patrimonii titulo* . . . ad omnes, etiam sacros et presbyteratus ordines promoveri . . . libere et licite valeant, indulgemus . . ." Many [76] and Augustine [77] hold that this title was first granted by Urban VIII in 1631. Authors generally point to the origin of the *titulus missionis* under Gregory XIII.[78] Hinschius notes that the expression *titulus missionis* appears for the first time in the Brief of Urban VIII, April 12, 1631.[79] When the College of the Propaganda was founded Urban VIII granted the privilege of this title to its future students.[80] All students at their entrance into an in-

[73] Hinschius, *System des Kathol. Kirchenrechts*, I, p. 76.

[74] O. Mejer, *De Titulo Missionis Apud Catholicos*, Regiomonti, 1848, p. 13.

[75] *Bullarium Magnum* 2, 459.

[76] Many, *De Sacra Ordinatione*, n. 145.

[77] Augustine, *A Commentary on the New Code of Canon Law*, St. Louis, 1920, IV, p. 472.

[78] Hinschius, *System des Kathol. Kirchenrechts*, I, p. 76; Wernz, *Jus Decretalium*, II, n. 91; Honorante, *Praxis Secretariae Tribunalis*, Secunda Editio, Romae, 1762, cap. XVII, p. 171.

[79] Hinschius, *System des Kathol. Kirchenrechts*, I, p. 76, note 5.

[80] Urban VIII, Breve, "Ad Uberes Fructus ", May 18, 1638,—*Bullarium Pontificium Sacrae Congregationis de Propaganda Fidei*, Romae, 1839, Tomus I, 91.

stitute which enjoyed this privilege had to oblige themselves under oath to serve the missions for life.[81] They were to receive their sustenance from the Institutes dependent upon the Congregation of the Propaganda. This extraordinary title of ordination which nearly always derived its canonical force from a special Apostolic Indult and from the oath of the ordinand may be defined as follows: " Titulus missionis consistit in ipso iure quo fruuntur clerici (hoc tituli ordinati), ut ex ministerio, cui addicti sunt vel addicentur in hac vel illa missione, ad victum necessaria consequantur." [82] The cleric had to take the oath. This was the usual title to which the clergy of the United States were ordained until 1908.[83]

2. TITULUS SERVITII ECCLESIAE

Closely akin to the title of mission is the *titulus servitii ecclesiae*. This is also a supplementary title. Essentially it does not differ from the title of mission. The Fathers of the Vatican Council in the schema " *de titulis ordinationum* " considered the introduction of the title of service of the Church.[84] " . . . .Decernimus . . . et si nec ita patrimonium haberi possit, eosdem episcopi ordinent titulo servitii suae diocesis seu ecclesiae, et de ecclesiastico officio provideant, quo decenter sustentari valeant."

Although no immediate action was taken upon this propositum of the Vatican Fathers with regard to the *titulus ad servitium ecclesiae* (or sometimes called *titulus mensae episcopalis*) it began to be practically recognized.[85] The Plenary Council of Latin America mentioned the *titulus servitii ecclesiae* in the title " de Sacramentis " chapter seven.[86] This title found incorporation in the new Code of Canon Law.[87]

[81] *Bullar. Propag.* I, 140-141. [82] Many, *De Sacra Ordinatione*, n. 145.

[83] Augustine, *Commentary*, IV, p. 472; Conc. Pl. Balt. II, n. 323; Conc. Pl. Balt. III, n. 165.

[84] *Acta et Decreta Sacrorum Conciliorum Recentiorum*, Collectio Lacensis, Friburgi Brisgoviae, 1890, Tomus Septimus, p. 669.

[85] Peries, " Titulus Ordinationis," *A. E. R.*, 13 (1895), 353.

[86] *Acta et Decreta Concilii Plenarii Americae Latinae*, 1900, p. 254, n. 582: " Secluso speciali indulto, nemo ad sacros Ordines promoveri potest nisi

3. TITULUS MENSAE

A few years after the Council of Trent the *titulus mensae* made its appearance in Germany.[88] This title was contrary to the common law and necessitated a special indult according to papal documents.[89] It originated because of the weakening of the title of pension in Germany,[90] and was very much similar to the *titulus paupertatis.* Many [91] gives as a definition the following: "Titulus mensae communis consistit in ipso iure, quod unusquisque religiosus, vi suae professionis votorum simplicium, adipiscitur, nempe ut sustentetur ex bonis monasterii seu congregationis, in qua vota emittit." Today the Code of Canon Law recognizes "for religious with simple perpetual vows, the title of *mensa communis,* or *congregationis,* or a similar one according to their constitutions." [92]

titulo ecclesiastico vel patrimoniali de honesta provisus sit. In nostris autem regionibus sufficit titulus administrationis seu ministerii sive servitii ecclesiae, iuxta Decretum Sacrae Congregationis, diei 21 Junii, 1879 quod in Appendice inserendum jussimus."—*A. S. S.*, 12, 569; Conc. Pl. Balt. III, p. 206.

[87] Canon 981, § 1.

[88] Synod of Augsburg, 1567, p. II, cap. 9.—Hartzheim 7, 177. Synod of Brixen, 1603. De Ministris Ecclesiae, eorumque officiis, n. 2: "Nullus ordinetur posthac sine beneficio, aut patrimonio, aut pensione . . . , aut denique sine titulo mensae, eoque perpetuo."—Hartzheim 8, 551. Synod of Chur, 1605,—Hartzheim 8, 650. Synod of Prague, 1605, tit. 22,—Hartzheim 8, 723.

[89] Pius IX, Bulla, "*Apostolicae Sedis*", Oct. 12, 1869, De Suspensionibus, n. 4,—*A. S. S.*, 5, 287-312. Pius V, Bulla, "*Romanus Pontifex Sacrorum*", Oct. 14, 1568,—*Fontes,* n. 299. "*Auctis Admodum*", Nov. 4, 1892, Decretum S. Congregationis Episcoporum et Regularium,—*Fontes,* n. 2020.

[90] Reiffenstuel, *Jus Canonicum Universum*, Parisiis, 1864, Lib. I, Tit. IX, n. 76.

[91] *De Sacra Ordinatione*, n. 189.

[92] Canon 982, § 2.

CHAPTER TWO

Proper Bishop of Ordination

The discussion of the proper bishop for ordination in this historical conspectus is closely linked with the foregoing consideration of the title of ordination. This connection exists because the early concept of the ordination title included the idea of a proper bishop for ordination. At ordination a cleric was ascribed permanently to a certain church. No one was to be ordained without this inscription. In this act of ascription one finds a basis for the idea of a proper bishop for ordination in the early Church. The study of the relation between ordination and ascription of the clerics embraces the competency of the minister who conferred Orders.[1]

Before considering the competency of the minister of Orders it will be well to point out who is the minister of Orders. A validly consecrated bishop is the ordinary and qualified minister of all Orders, both minor and major.[2] The bishop has the power to confer Orders because of episcopal consecration. Besides this power he needs also the right to confer Orders which fully qualifies him as the competent minister. To be the proper bishop for ordination means therefore, to enjoy both the power and the right to ordain.

The right to confer Orders flows from jurisdiction. The Pope as bishop of the entire world has full power of supreme jurisdiction.[3] He may ordain any one, anywhere and at any

[1] Fuchs, *Ordinationstitel*, p. 11ff.

[2] Council of Trent, Sess. XXIII, *de sacramento ordinis*, cap. 4, can. 7; c. 1, D. XXV; c. 4, D. LXVIII; c. 24, D. XCIII; Schmalzgrueber, *Jus Ecclesiasticum*, lib. I, tit. XI, n. 30; Decretum Eugenii IV pro Armenis,—Mansi 31, 1058; Denzinger, H.–Bannwart, C., *Enchiridion Symbolorum*, 18-20 ed., Friburgi Brisgoviae, 1932, n. 695: "Ordinarius minister huius sacramenti (ordinis) est episcopus."

[3] Canon 219.

time.[4] It is within his right to reserve the administration of any Order to himself if he so wishes. Since the Constitution "In Postremo", Oct. 25, 1756 of Benedict XIV [5] the regulation that it is unlawful to confer higher Orders on a man ordained by the Roman Pontiff without special faculty from the Holy See has received a permanent place in ecclesiastical law.[6]

Every other ordinary minister of ordination has limited jurisdiction. He is restricted in the use of his power to ordain. This limitation of his power through lack of jurisdiction is fundamental to the concept of the proper bishop for ordination.

It has been stated before that the ordination title in the early Church is intimately joined to the idea of *episcopus proprius*. This relationship will appear more convincingly against the historical background now to follow.

Christ before His ascension into heaven said to His disciples: "Go ye into the whole world and preach the gospel to every creature." [7] After His ascension the Apostles "going forth preached everywhere." [8] The limits of their field was the whole world. They set about their work of evangelizing, teaching the people and founding churches. The Apostles also created bishops to whose care they commended the newly founded churches. St. Paul left Titus at Crete that he "set in order the things that are wanting and ordain priests in every city." [9] Upon the death of the Apostles and during the first centuries of the Christian era bishops ordained men who were not their subjects or went into other cities to ordain and to govern. Because of these disciplinary disturbances the early Councils strictly forbade bishops to exercise their powers outside their own territory. They were not to confer Orders in the territory of another bishop without his permission.

[4] Gasparri, *De Sacra Ordinatione*, n. 792.

[5] *Fontes*, n. 442.

[6] Canon 952; Ferraris, *Prompta Bibliotheca Canonica*, Parisiis, 1865, "ordo" art. III, n. 86.

[7] Mark 16: 15.

[8] Mark 16: 20.

[9] Titus 1: 5.

Neither were they to ordain men who were not their subjects. The canons of these Councils in making regulations limiting the powers of the bishops established a proper bishop for ordination. Thus canon 17 of the Council of Arles, 314, said that a bishop was not to molest another bishop. Hefele [10] explains that one manner of molestation consisted in entering another diocese and while there performing pontifical functions, particularly ordaining subjects of the second bishop. Likewise canon 16 of the Council of Nice, 325: " Sin autem etiam ausus fuerit quispiam eum, qui ad alium pertinet surripere, et in ecclesia, non consetiente proprio episcopo, a quo recessit qui in canone censetur, irrita fuit ordinatio." [11] In a letter of Pope Julius I (336-352) written probably in 341 to the Oriental bishops a similar prohibition was mentioned.[12] Again canons 13 and 22 of the Council of Antioch, 341, contained this legislation.[13] Canon 3 of this same Council referred to the *episcopus proprius* who should recall a cleric who had left his *parochia*.[14] The Council of Sardica, 347, dealt with this matter in canons 18 and 19.[15] These were joined into one in the *Corpus Juris Canonici*.[16]

10 Hefele 1, 214; Mansi 2, 473.

11 Mansi 2, 675; Hefele 1, 420; c. 3, D. LXXI.

12 N. 6: " Nullus episcopus alterius parochianum praesumat retinere, aut ordinare absque eius episcopi voluntate, vel iudicare, salva tamen in omnibus apostolica auctoritate: quia sicut irrita erit eius ordinatio ita et dijudicatio." —Mansi 2, 1185; Canon 36 of the Apostolic Canons,—Hefele 1, 811; Mansi 1, 35.

13 " Nullus episcopus ex alia provincia audeat ad aliam transgredi ad promotionem ministerii aliquos in ecclesiis ordinare, licet consensum videantur praebere nonnulli nisi literis tam metropolitani quam ceterorum qui cum eo sunt episcoporum rogatus adveniat, et sic ad actionem ordinationis accedat." —Mansi 2, 1323; Hefele 1, 517. " Episcopus alienam civitatem quae non est illi subjecta, non adeat; nec ad possessionem accedat quae ad eum pertinet super ordinationem cuiusquam; nec constituat presbyteros, aut diaconos alteri subjectos episcopi, nisi forte consilio et voluntate regionis episcopi."—Mansi 2, 1326; Hefele 1, 519-520.

14 Mansi 2, 1310; Hefele 1, 514.

15 Mansi 6, 1150; Hefele 1, 597.

16 C. 1, D. LXXI.

It seems that after the fourth century and for the following five centuries no special regulation was made with regard to a proper bishop of ordination for a lay person. Thomassinus [17] considers the ordinations of laymen such as Origen, Augustine, Jerome and Paulinus (referred to above). As has been seen they were ordained by bishops (not their proper bishops) without permission of their proper bishops. Even though no objections were raised by their own bishops it is clear from the first chapter that their ordinations were absolute ordinations which the Councils reprobated. It is the opinion of Thomassinus that any bishop could ordain lay persons. Hinschius [18] takes exception to this opinion. He says that individual canons [19] presupposed the rule that the ordinand belonged to the diocese of the ordaining prelate thus making the bishop of domicile competent. Before ordination every candidate had to be thoroughly examined by the bishop who was to impose hands. From the regulations it appears that the principle of the law (every ordinand must have a proper bishop whether lay or cleric) was contained in the very nature of the qualifications of a candidate. The universality of the law can hardly be doubted. It also embraced lay persons.

Some texts seem to claim that baptism gave the bishop competence to confer Orders upon lay persons because baptism was generally administered in the domicile of the person.[20] In the early centuries adults received baptism only after some time of residence and instruction. Through baptism one became a

[17] *Vetus et Nova Ecclesiae Disciplina*, P. II, lib. I, cap. I, n. 2-12; *ibidem*, cap. II-VI.

[18] *System des Kathol. Kirchenrechts*, I, p. 86.

[19] C. 6, D. LXXI; c. 5 of the First Council of Carthage, 348,—Mansi 3, 155; c. 1 of the Council of Sardica, 347, is likewise given this interpretation,—Mansi 3, 6; c. 1, X, *de clericis non residentibus in ecclesia vel praebenda*, III, 4.

[20] Canon 24 of the Council of Elvira, 306,—Mansi 2, 10; Hefele 1, 165; c. 4, D. XCVIII. Augustine says that baptism constituted the first title for the competency of the bishop. Since baptism, he says, in the first four centuries was conferred on adults by the bishop himself, it was but natural that the spiritual father had the first claim on the persons thus regenerated. —*Commentary* IV, p. 418.

member of a certain parish. Hinschius does not arrive at a definite conclusion.[21] He maintains that the few examples cited by Thomassinus cannot be advanced as a law.[22] It is quite certain that the examples of absolute ordinations in the ancient Church do not prove that lay persons had no proper bishop of ordination for centuries.

RESTRICTION OF JURISDICTION

In order to avoid confusion and in order to keep unworthy men out of the ranks of the clergy the jurisdiction of every bishop was limited to a definite territory. No bishop could licitly confer Orders outside his own territory nor ordain men not his subjects. Neither could he confer Orders upon those not his subjects within his own territory.[23]

A review of the various canons of the Councils will effectively demonstrate the sound and salutary legislation which obtained in the first centuries of the Church. They will serve to show in what manner the bishops' jurisdiction was restricted and how this restriction brought out the idea of a proper bishop for ordination.

[21] *System des Kathol. Kirchenrechts*, I, p. 86, n. 6.

[22] Wernz is of the opinion that the legislation likewise extended to lay persons.—*Jus Decretalium*, II, n. 26. Canon 16 of the Council of Rome, 402, stated that lay persons who have been excluded from Orders by their own bishop may not be received into the ranks of the clergy elsewhere.—Mansi 3, 1139; Hefele 2, 88.

[23] Special note on the word "diocese".

The expression παροικία occurs in canon 16 of the Council of Nice, 325, and in Canons 14 and 15 of the Apostolic Canons. The expression *parochia* together with *parochianus* were found in the Occident to denote diocese and diocesan (C. 4, C. X, q. 1; c. 10, C. IX, q. 2). In the West they more frequently designated parish and parishioner.

The expression διοίκησις which appeared in the Orient at the Council of Constantinople, 381, (canon 2,—Mansi 3, 559) was accepted in Africa (C. 50, 51, C. XVI, q. 1).

Occasionally the Occident used the word "diocese" for parish or parish church (C. 3, C. XII, q. 4). In canon 35 of the Council of Toledo, 633,—Mansi 10, 628-629, the word was used as the specific name for diocese (C. 11, C. X, q. 1). Since the fifth century the word "diocese" has been used generally in the sense in which it is employed today.

The force of the quotations from the Councils up to the Council of Trent will help to convey a clearer and more authentic historical conspectus of the proper bishop for ordination. They are given here as a direct aid to this study.

They regulated: 1) That a bishop shall not ordain a candidate who is not his subject without the permission of the bishop to whom the candidate belongs.[24] 2) That a bishop shall not

[24] Canon 6 of the Council of Rome, 386: "Ut de aliena ecclesia ordinare clericum nullus usurpet."—Mansi 3, 670; Hefele 2, 46. Canon 8 of the First Council of Orange, 441,—Mansi 6, 437; Hefele 2, 293. Canon 21 of the Third Council of Carthage, 397: "Ut clericum alienum nisi concedente eius episcopo, nemo audeat, vel retinere, vel promovere in ecclesia sibi."—Mansi 3, 883-884; c. 2, D. LXXII. Canon 6 of the Council of Telepte, 418: "Clericum alienum nullus audeat ordinare."—Mansi 4, 380. Letter of St. Leo the Great to Anastasius, 446, cap. 9: "Alienum clericum, invito episcopo ipsius nemo suscipiat, nemo sollicitet: nisi forte ex placito caritatis id inter dantem accipientemque convenerit."—Mansi 5, 1183. Letter of St. Leo the Great to the Metropolitans in the provinces of Illyria, 446, cap. 4: "Illud quoque pari observantia ad sacerdotalis concordiae vinculum ab omnibus volumus custodiri, ut nullus episcopus alterius episcopi clericum sibi audeat vindicare, sine illius ad quem pertinet cessione, quam tamen evidentia scripta contineant..."—Mansi 5, 1175. Canon 9 of the Council of Angers, 453.—Mansi 7, 901; Hefele 2, 582. Canon 13 of the Second Council of Arles, 452: "Quod si aliquo commorationis tempore, invito episcopo suo, in aliena ecclesia habitans ab episcopo loci clericus fuerit ordinatus, huiusmodi ordinatio irrita habeatur."—Mansi 7, 880; Hefele 2, 300. Canon 10 of the Council of Vennes, 465.—Mansi 7, 954; Hefele 2, 594. Caput 6 of the Council of Valencia, 524,—Mansi 8, 622; Hefele 2, 710. Canon 10 of the Council of Auvergne, 535,—Mansi 8, 861; Hefele 2, 762. Canon 13 of the Council of Chalon, 650: "Ut nullus alterius clericum retinere praesumat, sicut priscis est canonibus statutum, nec ad sacrum ordinem sine voluntate episcopi sui penitus promovere."—Mansi 10, 1192. Caput 8 of the Council of Ratisbon, 788: "Ut clericum nemo recipere audeat sine consensu episcopi sui..."—Mansi 17B, 208. Canons 14 and 15 of the Council of Mainz, 888, —Mansi 18A, 68; Hefele 4, 548; Harduin 6A, 408-410; Hartzheim 2, 373. Canon 9 of the Council of Rouen, 1050: "Ut episcopus alterius diocesis clericum nisi sub legatione, aut probabilibus signis, ordinare praesumat."—Mansi 19, 753; Harduin 6A, 1012. Canon 10 of the Council of London, 1125: "Nullus episcoporum alterius praesumat parochianum ordinare aut judicare: unusquisque enim suo domino stat aut cadit: nec tenetur aliquis sententia non a sua judice prolata."—Harduin 6B, 1126. Canon 10 of the Council of Rouen, 1231,—Mansi 23, 215; Hefele 5, 100. Canon 15 of the Second Council of Lyons, 1274,—Mansi 24, 91; Hefele 6, 149; c. 2, *de temporibus ordinationum et qualitate ordinandorum*, I, 9 in VI. Canon 9 of the

enter the diocese of another bishop and while there confer Orders, nor shall he accept candidates into his own diocese without the permission of their bishop.[25] 3) That the candidates for Orders shall be subject to an examination.[26] 4) That

Council of Cologne, 1279: "Item omnes illi, qui ordinem aliquem sacrum vel non sacrum ab alienis Episcopis receperint, nostra super hoc speciali licentia non obtenta, executionem Ordinis sibi noverint interdictam."—Mansi 24, 356; Hefele 6, 204. Canon 5 of the Council of Aquileja, 1282,—Mansi 24, 434; Hefele 6, 228.

[25] Cap. II of the Council of Constantinople, 381: "Qui sunt super dioecesim episcopi, nequaquam ad ecclesias, quae sunt extra praefixos sibi terminos, accedant, nec eas hac praesumptione confundant."—Mansi 3, 566-567; Hartzheim 1, 167. Canon 20 of the Third Council of Carthage, 397: "Placuit ut a nullo episcopo usurpentur plebes alienae, nec aliquis episcoporum supergrediatur in dioecesi suum collegam."—Mansi 3, 883. Canon 20 of the Council of Chalcedon, 451: "Clericos in sua ecclesia existentes sicut jam definivimus, non licere in alterius civitate ordinari, et ecclesia; sed contentos in illa esse in qua ministrare ab initio meruerunt praeter illos qui perdiderunt suas patrias, et donec in alteram ecclesiam transierunt."—Mansi 6, 1228. Canon 9 of the Council of Tours, 461,—Mansi 7, 946; Hefele 2, 589. Canon 4 of the Council of Lyons, 517,—Mansi 8, 569; Hefele 2, 688. Canon 15 of the Third Council of Orleans, 538: "Episcopus in dioeceses alienas ad alienos clericos ordinandos vel consecranda altaria irruere non debet."—Mansi 9, 16; Hefele 2, 776. Canons 2 and 5 of the Council of Hereford, 673,—Mansi 11, 129; Hefele 3, 113. Caput II of the Capitularia Regum Francorum, Aachen, 789: "Item in eodem Concilio [Antiocheno] simul et in Sardicensi, necnon et in Decretalibus Innocentii Papae, ut nullus episcopus in alterius parochia ordinationes aliquas audeat facere, vel negotia peragere quae ad eum non pertinent."—Mansi 17B, 217; Hartzheim 1, 269. Capitulary of Theodulfus, Bishop of Orleans, to the priests of his diocese, 797, cap. 15: "Hoc quoque modis omnibus prohibemus, ut nullus vestrum alterius clericum sollicitet aut recipiat quia gravis de hac re in sacris canonibus sententia est."—Mansi 13, 998. Canon 18 of the Capitula Hadriani Papae, 785: "Nullus episcopus alterius parochianum praesumat retinere, aut ordinare absque eius voluntate vel judicare."—Hartzheim 1, 253. Canon 3 of the Council of Ravenna, 997, "... Tamen competere non ambiguimus ut praesenti concilio priscorum Patrum sanctiones firmantes teneamus, ut nemo nostrum ecclesiam vel aliquando Oratorium in alterius Dioecesi dedicare attentet sine permissu et consensu Episcopi, ad quem pertinet ipsa Dioecesis; neque alterius Dioecesenses vel Parochianos recipere aut promovere seu retinere praesumat sine canonicis epistolis quas Nicaeae Synodus apud Bithyniam congregata sancivit latino more vocitari formatas."—Mansi 19, 220-221; Harduin 6A, 753-754. Canon 53 of the Council of Benevent, 1378,—Mansi 26, 646; Hefele 6, 939.

[26] Canon 20 of the Council of Hippo, 393: "Ut nullus ordinetur nisi probatus vel episcoporum examine vel populi testimonio."—Mansi 3, 922;

exempt religious shall receive Orders from the bishop in whose diocese they live.[27] 5) In reading the text of the canons one finds the frequent use of the terms, *suus episcopus, alienus episcopus, ordinarius suus, clericus alienus* and *absque licentia sui episcopi.* A few canons expressly employ the term *episcopus proprius.*[28] 6) The use of the above-mentioned terms and the force of the legislation indicate the existence of the concept of a proper bishop for ordination.

The canons of the Councils demonstrate the established discipline of the Church in the early centuries with respect to the proper bishop for ordination. The old discipline, particularly up to the twelfth century, considered the perpetual bond which held the cleric to a definite church. The cleric was bound to a certain church and was held to serve that church. The relation of the cleric to his bishop was elucidated in the ordination title treated above. Ascription in the ancient Church was the chief title for the competency of the proper bishop for ordination. Once this ascription was effected the bishop could promote the cleric to higher Orders. The cleric was considered to have his domicile at the church to which he was

Hefele 2, 57. Synod of Exeter, 1287: "Clerici ab alieno episcopo ordinati, non prius ad executionem sui ordinis in nostra dioecesi admittantur, donec de earum ordinatione, litteratura, conversatione, moribus nobis vel locorum archidiacono fidem fecerint manifestam."—Mansi 24, 797D. Canon 7 of the Council of Beziers, 1310: "Provideatur insuper ne aliquis tonsurandus ad clericatum vel ad ordines promovendus mittatur ab uno episcopo ad alium nisi fuerit per suum ordinarium examinatus, et ut dignus approbatus, de quibus in littera quam ad ordinatorem diriget, expressa mentio habeatur." —Mansi 25, 361.

[27] Canon 17 of the First General Council of the Lateran, 1123, stated that monks were to receive orders at the hands of the bishop in whose diocese they lived.—Mansi 21, 304; Hefele 5, 381. Rubric IV of the Council of Ravenna, 1314,—Mansi 25, 538; Hefele 6, 569. Canon 6 of the Council of Lambeth, 1330,—Mansi 25, 895; Hefele 6, 632.

[28] Canon 5 of the Council of Erfurt, 932,—Mansi 18A, 364; Harduin 6A, 574; Canon 5 of the Council of Poitiers, 1078: "Ut nullus Abbas, monachus vel quilibet alius poenitentias injungat nisi quibus proprius episcopus hanc curam dederit."—Harduin 6A, 1575. Canon 7 of the Council of London, 1138: "Clericos a non suis episcopis absque litteris proprii episcopi ordinatos a susceptorum officiis ordinum inhibemus."—Harduin 6B, 1204-1205.

ascribed. Another bishop could not ordain him without the permission of the proper bishop. Ordination itself ascribed the candidate to a certain church. The Bishop of that church was the proper bishop for ordination. This would seemingly exclude the lay person. It has been suggested that the lay person became ascribed to a church in virtue of baptism. The layman, indeed, was not appointed to a certain church for a definite service nevertheless he was a *parochianus,*[29] and had his own proper parish. The lay member of the parish could not leave without the bishop's permission.[30] The layman going from one church to another was commanded to have letters of commendation.[31] The ascription of a layman and of a cleric were of a different nature but in each instance they gave the person a proper bishop of ordination. Wernz [32] states that in the old law the bishop was the competent minister of ordination *sive ex titulo baptismi sive nativitatis spiritualis* or finally *ex titulo ordinationis.*

In the twelfth century the change in the ordination title effected a change as to the proper bishop. Besides the title of benefice identified with ascription there arose two other titles, i. e., of origin and of domicile. In view of these three titles a person could have had three proper bishops for ordination, the bishop of the place where the benefice was located, the bishop of origin and the bishop of domicile. It is uncertain when this change in the discipline took place.[33] No decree nor canon can be found prior to the Decretals of Boniface VIII by which the existence of this threefold title can be proven. The first legislation indicative of the change is mentioned in c. 1, *de temporibus ordinationum et qualitate ordinandorum,* I, 9 in VI.

[29] C. 10 of the Council of London, 1125,—Harduin 6B, 1126; c. 3 of the Council of Ravenna, 997,—Mansi 19, 220-221; Harduin 6A, 753-754.

[30] Thomassinus, *Vetus et Nova Ecclesiae Disciplina,* P. II, lib. I, cap. VII, n. 4.

[31] Lupus, *Opera Omnia Canonica,* Venetiis, 1727, T. IX, pp. 197-200; c. 7 of the Council of Antioch, 341,—Mansi 2, 1311; Hefele 1, 515.

[32] *Jus Decretalium,* II, n. 26.

[33] Van Espen, *Jus Ecclesiasticum Universum,* P. II, Sect. I, tit., n. 12.

This decretal of Clement IV in express words designated as proper bishops the bishop of origin and the bishop of benefice: "Statuimus ut nullus episcoporum Italiae de caetero aliquem ultramontanum clericum ordinare praesumat, nisi a Nobis specialem licentiam habeat vel ab episcopo de cuius diocesi traxit originem ordinandus vel in cuius diocesi beneficiatus existit, per eius patentes litteras causam rationabilem continentes quare ipsum nolit, aut nequeat ordinare." Hinchius points out that the first part of the decretal presupposed clearly that the place of origin and the place of domicile were considered identical.[34] Boniface VIII, 1299, definitely recognized the following bishops as proper bishops of ordination: bishop of origin, bishop of benefice and bishop of domicile. "Cum nullus Clericum Paroeciae alienae, praeter ipsius licentiam debeat ordinare; Superior intelligitur in hoc casu Episcopus, de cuius Dioecesi est is qui ad Ordines promoveri desiderat oriundus, seu in cuius Dioecesi Beneficium obtinet Ecclesiasticum, seu habet, licet alibi natus fuerit, domicilium in eadem. . . ."[35]

At the time of the convocation of the great Tridentine Council three proper bishops for ordination had common recognition. Somewhat prior to the Council of Trent a fourth proper bishop appeared, i. e., *ratione familiaritatis seu commensalitii.* No definite date can be given when this bishop first obtained the right of an *episcopus proprius.* The Council of Orange, 441, in canon 8 suggested the title of *familiaritas.*[36] The Glossa on canon 2, *de temporibus ordinationum et qualitate ordinandorum,* I, 9 in VI considers the word "*figmento*" an indication of *familiaritas* when it says "vel in fraudem constitutionis huius aliquem in familiarem recepit." The express approbation given to this title by the Council of Trent demonstrates clearly the existence of a custom prior to the Council.[37] *Fam-*

[34] *System des Kathol. Kirchenrechts,* I, p. 87.

[35] C. 3, *de temporibus ordinationum et qualitate ordinandorum,* I, 9 in VI.

[36] "Si quis alibi consistentem clericum ordinandum putaverit, prius definiat ut cum ipso habitet; sic quoque sine consultatione episcopi cum quo ante habitavit..., eum ordinare non praesumat."—Mansi 6, 437.

[37] Sess. XXIII, *de reformatione,* cap. 9: "Episcopus familiarem suum non subditum ordinare non possit, nisi per triennium secum fuerit commoratus,

iliares were those who lived with the bishop and who were subject to him. The bishop cared for them at his own expense. They were his domestic *commensales*.[38] No bishop was to ordain any of them unless they had lived with him for three years. Titular bishops were not proper bishops of ordination for their *familiares*.[39] The Council of Trent then definitely added this as a fourth title to the titles discernible in the Decretals, i. e. origin, domicile and benefice.[40]

The discipline confirmed by the Council of Trent merited greater confirmation and explanation by Innocent XII in the celebrated Constitution, *Speculatores,* November 5, 1694.[41] This document treats solely of the proper bishop for ordination. Its importance need hardly be stressed because it is an invaluable source and will find further application to this study in the second part of this dissertation. Suffice it to say here that Innocent XII enumerated and determined the requisites for an *episcopus proprius sive ratione originis sive ratione domicilii sive ratione beneficii sive ratione familiaritatis.*

A custom contrary to this Constitution soon became evident. It consisted in this that clerics, after they had been perpetually released by the bishop of the diocese to which they belonged, would present themselves to another bishop. They would take the oath required by Innocent XII in the Constitution *Speculatores* to remain in the second diocese. The bishop of the second diocese would ordain them as his own subjects even before they had resided in the new diocese for the length of time required by the Constitution. This custom created another proper bishop of ordination. On December 11, 1897 the Sacred Congregation of the Council was asked whether this

et beneficium quacunque fraude cessante statim re ipsa illi conferat; consuetudine quacunque, etiam immemorabili, in contrarium non obstante." Many refers to it as a *consuetudo longissima.—De Sacra Ordinatione,* n. 39.

38 C. 5, *de verborum significatione,* V, 12 in VI; Reiffenstuel, *Jus Canonicum Universum,* Lib. II, tit. 11, n. 99.

39 Sess. XIV, *de reformatione,* cap. 2.

40 Sess. XXIII, *de reformatione,* cap. 9.

41 *Fontes,* n. 258.

custom was legitimate. The response was "*Providetur per decretum.*" [42] On July 20, 1898 the Decree *A Primis* was issued.[43] This decree dealt chiefly with the incardination and excardination of clerics. It did establish another title for a proper bishop. Incardination was that new title whereby one could obtain a proper bishop for ordination. The rules laid down in the Decree *A Primis* had to be observed if incardination was to constitute a bishop competent for ordination. No other form of incardination could be employed.[44] The Decree demanded a written document of absolute and perpetual excardination and incardination.[45] This form of incardination was adopted from the Decrees of the Third Plenary Council of Baltimore, 1884.[46]

No further legislation was enacted for the proper bishop of ordination of secular clerics until the promulgation of the Code of Canon Law. Before the Code then, a bishop became competent to ordain a man either *ratione domicilii,* or *ratione originis,* or *ratione beneficii,* or *ratione familiaritatis,* or *ratione incardinationis.*

EPISCOPUS PROPRIUS ORDINATIONIS QUOAD REGULARES

At the very beginning of the religious state the ordination of monks was reserved to the bishop of the diocese in which the monastery of the candidate was located.[47] Since in the first centuries of the Church regulars were subject to episcopal jurisdiction [48] they were also subject to the bishops in matters of

[42] *A. K. K. R.*, 79 (1899), 101.

[43] *Fontes*, n. 4307.

[44] S. Cong. Conc., Romana et aliarum, September 15, 1906—*A. S. S.*, 39 (1906), 498-499; *A. E. R.*, 35 (1906), 515.

[45] "Incardinationem faciendum esse ab episcopo non oretenus, sed in scriptis, absolute et in perpetuum."—S. Congr. Conc., decr. *A Primis*, July 20, 1898—*A. S. S.*, 31 (1898-1899), 49 ff.; *A. E. R.*, 20 (1899), 179; Canoniste 21 (1898), 678.

[46] *Acta et Decreta Concilii Plenarii Baltimorensis* III, n. 63.

[47] Many, *De Sacra Ordinatione*, n. 156.

[48] Mathis, Burkhard, O.M.Cap., *Die Privilegien des Franziskaner Ordens bis zum Konzil von Vienne* (1311), Paderborn, 1927, p. 1; Wernz, *Jus Decretalium*, II, n. 26; c. 12, C. XVI, q. 1; c. 10, C. XVIII, q. 2.

ordination. In 589 Gregory the Great ascended the papal throne. He was the first monk to become Pope. Certain minor privileges were granted to the monks by him upon the approbation of the rule of St. Benedict of Nursia.

In the course of the following centuries the Popes granted exemption to various monasteries. Everywhere, however, monks were subject to the local bishops in the reception of Orders. Small wonder then that canon 14 of the Fourth Council of Carthage, 401,[49] threatened the bishop with the penalty of excommunication if he unlawfully ordained a monk of another monastery, i. e., of another diocese. Likewise in canon 80 of the Council of Carthage, 419,[50] the penalty of excommunication was mentioned for the bishop and the penalty of deposition for the monk. The early Church recognized grave dangers to the religious state if the monk were ordained without permission of the bishop and without consent of the superior (Abbot).[51] Because of these dangers the Council of Agde [52] and the Council of Lerida [53] insisted on the consent and permission of the Abbot or on the presentation of the candidate by the Abbot for ordination to the bishop. The canons of these Councils passed into the common law under Lucius III (1181-1185).[54] In 1123 the First Council of the Lateran decreed that all pontifical functions necessary to monasteries were to be performed by the diocesan bishop.[55]

The extensive growth and activity of the Mendicant Orders during the thirteenth century necessitated special legislation.

[49] Mansi 3, 971; Hefele 2, 84.

[50] Canon 80 in Codice Canonum Ecclesiae Africanae—Mansi 3, 779.

[51] C. 5, X, *de temporibus ordinationum et qualitate ordinandorum*, I, 11.

[52] Canon 27 of the Council of Agde, 506,—Mansi 8, 329; Hefele 2, 654; c. 12, C. XVIII, q. 2.

[53] Canon 3 of the Council of Lerida, 524,—Mansi 8, 612; Hefele 2, 705; c. 34, C. XVI, q. 1.

[54] C. 5, X, *de temporibus ordinationum et qualitate ordinandorum*, I, 11.

[55] Canon 17: "Interdicimus abbatibus et monachis publicas poenitentias dare, et infirmos visitare, et unctiones facere, et missas publicas cantare. Chrisma et oleum consecrationes altarium ordinationes clericorum ab episcopis accipiant in quorum parochiis manent."—Mansi 21, 285; Hefele 5, 381.

Friars were often transferred from monastery to monastery and consequently did not always remain in the one diocese. To facilitate their reception of Orders, Clement IV (1265-1268) privileged the superiors to present their subjects for ordination to any bishop in communion with the Holy See.[56] Sixtus IV, 1474, confirmed this privilege in his Constitution *Regimini Universalis*[57] and later either by direct concession or by communication of privileges it was extended to other religious orders.[58]

In 1536 Leo X issued a Bull concerning the privileges of religious which restricted the former privileges.[59] The Council of Trent further revoked the privileges of regulars.[60] Immediately a controversy arose whether the Council had recalled the privilege of regulars to receive Orders from any bishop. Pius V, in his Constitution, *Etsi Mendicantium,* May 16, 1567[61] declared that the regulations of the Council did not affect the regulars. Gregory XIII, the successor of St. Pius V, in his Constitution, "*In tanta rerum*", March 1, 1573,[62] insisted that the regulations of the Council of Trent did affect the regulars. In the same year (1573) Gregory XIII declared that Carthusian monks, who had asked to be ordained by another bishop, were obliged to seek the permission of their proper bishop, i. e., of the bishop in whose diocese the monastery

[56] Const., *Virtute Conspicuos,* July 21, 1265—*Bullarium Magnum,* Luxemburgi, 1727, T. I, 137-138; *Bullarium Romanum,* T. I, pars I, 433.

[57] *Bull. M.*, T. I, 393.

[58] Wernz, *Jus Decretalium,* II, n. 27; Many, *De Sacra Ordinatione,* n. 156.

[59] *Bull. M.*, T. I, 582; Mansi 32, 972E; Hefele 8, 715.

[60] Sess. VII, *de reformatione,* cap. 11; Sess. XXIII, *de reformatione,* cap. 8.

[61] *Fontes,* n. 121.

[62] *Bull. R.*, T. VIII, p. 39: "Haec Bulla est reductio ad terminos juris communis et concilii Tridentini trium constitutionum a Pio V pro Ordinibus Mendicantium aliisque editarum." The three are: *Etsi Mendicantium,* May 16, 1567, which was mentioned above. *Ad Exequendum,* November 1, 1567, —*Bull. R.*, T. VII, 628-630 and *Romani Pontifices,* August 6, 1571—*Bull. R.*, T. VII, 938-939.

was located.[63] Sixtus V defined that the superior of regulars had the right to grant dimissorial letters to his subjects but only to the diocesan bishop, unless he were absent or would not ordain.[64] Finally Clement VIII, 1596, issued a Decree in which he further confirmed the Sistine Decree.[65] Innocent XIII in a Bull, *Apostolici Ministerii*,[66] and Benedict XIV in the Constitution, *Impositi Nobis*, gave further authentic interpretation of the Clementine Decree.

The Constitution, *Impositi Nobis*, dealt with the ordination of regulars. It gave the norms for the proper bishop of ordination of regulars up to the time of the Code of Canon Law. The important legislation of this Constitution can be summarized as follows:

1. The superior of regulars had the right to grant to his subjects dimissorial letters. The word *praesentatio* was often used in the place of *dimissio* of subjects. The meaning of both words was the same.

2. Ordinarily these dimissorial letters were to be addressed to the diocesan bishop, that is, to the bishop of the diocese in which the religious house was situated. In paragraph 15 of the Constitution, *Impositi Nobis*, Benedict XIV called attention to the fraudulent procedure on the part of the superiors who moved their subjects to a certain religious house at the time of ordination and immediately after the reception of Orders had them returned to the first religious house.

3. Two exceptions obtained when, a) the diocesan bishop was absent from his diocese and b) when the bishop of the

[63] Benedict XIV referred to this Decree in his Constitution, *Impositi Nobis*, par. 3, March 4, 1747—*Bull. R. Continuata*, II, 164-170.

[64] The Decree of Sixtus V is contained in the Const., *Impositi Nobis*, of Benedict XIV, February 27, 1747—*Fontes*, n. 376.

[65] The Decree of Clement VIII is also found in the Const., *Impositi Nobis*, of Benedict XIV.

[66] May 23, 1723—*Bull. R.*, T. XXI, 931-942. Innocent XIII directed this Bull to the Church in Spain, later on it was extended to the entire Church by Benedict XIV in the Const., *Impositi Nobis*. Pope Benedict XIII had specifically confirmed the Bull of Innocent XII in his Constitution, *In Supremo*, September 23, 1724—*Fontes*, n. 283.

diocese did not confer Orders even though he was in his diocese. A third exception existed when the see was vacant.

4. In these cases of exception the superior could send his subjects to any bishop provided a) the superior did so without fraud; b) the superior stated in the dimissorials why he was sending his subject to another bishop (either because the diocesan bishop was absent or would not confer Orders); c) the superior had to have an authentic statement of the absence of the bishop or of the fact that he would not ordain.

5. The superior of regulars had the right to grant dimissorials to his professed subjects for every Order from first tonsure to priesthood inclusive. The decrees made no distinction.

6. Superiors who acted contrary to the above laws incurred a twofold privation, i. e., one of office and dignity, the other of active and passive voice in the order. Benedict XIV declared that these penalties were *latae sententiae* in paragraph 11 of the Constitution, *Impositi Nobis*. Bishops who violated the regulations incurred the suspension imposed by the Council of Trent.[67]

7. It has been stated above that regulars before the Council of Trent generally enjoyed the privilege of sending or presenting their subjects to any bishop in communion with the Holy See. To others this privilege was directly granted while others received the privilege by communication. The Council of Trent suppressed all these privileges. Soon after the Council religious orders sought a renewal of privileges. Gregory XIII on September 22, 1582 in his Brief [68] *Pium et Utile* made concessions anew to the Society of Jesus. Because of this Benedict XIV in his Constitution, *Impositi Nobis,* gave the following norms:

a) Privileges no longer existed if they had been granted before the Tridentine Council and had not been confirmed after the Council *in forma specifica.*

[67] Sess. XXIII, *de reformatione*, cap. 8; Sess. XIV, *de reformatione*, cap. 2.

[68] *Bull. R.*, T. VII, 397-398.

b) Privileges granted after the Council were valid only when granted to the orders *nominatim atque directe.* The privilege to receive Orders at the hands of any bishop was incommunicable.

The regulations for the ordinations of regulars as contained in the Constitution, *Impositi Nobis,* remained in force up to the Code of Canon Law. As will be seen many of these regulations were incorporated into the Code. In 1888 a doubt was submitted to the Sacred Congregation of the Council which accentuated the legal force of the Constitution, *Impositi Nobis.* The doubt: "*an consuetudo contraria ab illa constitutione Benedictina derogare possit in casu*" received a negative answer.[69] In the *votum consultoris* which preceded the response this matter was given the following consideration: "Nulla enim opus est consuetudine ubi diserte privilegium illud intra statutos limites in ipsa Benedictina constitutione asseritur. Si vero consuetudo inducta fuisset ut neque illi limites servarentur, puto eam non esse consuetudinem sed corruptelam, quaeque nervum disrumperet ecclesiasticae disciplinae."

[69] *Thesaurus Resolutionum S. C. C.,* T. 147, 600; *A. S. S.,* 21, 359-365.

CHAPTER THREE

Dimissorial Letters in the Early Church

In the early Church clerics were ordained for a particular post, they were ordained with a title. No one could sever the bond which held them to their own church except the bishop who had so ordained them. They were not to leave without the consent of their proper bishop. A cleric, therefore, who wished to go to another church sought dismissal from his own bishop. If the bishop consented, letters would be drawn up by which the bishop signified that he absolved the cleric from ascription to his church. The bishop would dismiss the cleric, relinquish him to a second bishop and transfer the rights he had over the cleric to the bishop receiving him. These letters were rightly called *litterae dismissoriae* from the Latin word *dimittere*.[1] This signification of the words was the accepted meaning. They were rather letters of excorporation or excardination.[2] Gratian reproduced such letters as examples of those composed by the Fathers of the Council of Nice, 325.[3]

[1] "Dimissoriae Litterae, inquit, Modestinus, sunt, quae vulgo *apostoli* dicuntur, quod per eas causa ad eum qui appelatus est, dimittitur." — Forcellini, *Lexicon*, T. 2, p. 86; Dig. 50, 16, 106.

[2] Many, *De Sacra Ordinatione*, n. 60.

[3] ". . . Ego, inquam Burchardus humilis episcopus, in nomine Patris, et Filii, et Spiritus sancti, et in unitate solvendi, absolvo Hermannum presbyterum de civitate Wormaciensi indictione X, et licentiam do vobis inthronizandi eum in quacumque ecclesia vultis vestrae parochiae."—C. 1, D. LXXIII.

"... cuius voluntati consentientes secundum auctoritatem litteras ei dimissorias dedimus, per quas et ipsi concedimus, ut sub vestro magisterio divinae servituti insistens suae deserviat utilitati, et vobis licentiam tribuimus, ut, si dignum eum iudicaveritis, ad sacros ordines promoveatis. Commendatum ergo eum curae vestrae suscipite, et nostris ex partibus absolutum in vestrarum ovium numero custodite."—C. 2, D. LXXIII; c. 16 of the Council of Nice,—Mansi 2, 675.

The canons of the early Councils verify the common acceptation of the words " dimissorial letters " which prevailed in the ancient Church. No bishop could take unto his church a cleric who was ascribed to another without the dimissorials of the proper bishop.[4] The dimissorials were required not only for the ordination of a cleric by another bishop but in order that the cleric could be attached to another church. The custom of the times did not permit a cleric to be ascribed to another church until he had been dismissed from the church to which he had been previously attached. The dimissorial letters served this purpose.[5] It must be noted that the dismissorials of today are generally, one can say, always *litterae temporales.* The bishop or religious superior who issues them retains his first right and authority over the cleric. This concept was foreign to the ancient Church because of the perpetual ascription to the church which was linked with ordination. In the early centuries when a bishop allowed a member of his church or diocese to be ordained by the bishop of another he did so by means of *dimissoriae litterarae perpetuae.* These letters granted the cleric permanent release. He was free to go from his own diocese to another diocese. The execution of these letters was therefore rather an excardination and incardination than a sending of a cleric to another bishop for the reception of Orders. This mode of procedure, as is readily seen was a consequence of the legislation on the title of ordination. After the twelfth century (in this century came the change of ordination title)

[4] Canon 5 of the Council of Carthage, 341,—Hefele 1, 633; canon 21 of the Third Council of Carthage, 347: " Ut clericum alienum nisi concedente eius episcopo, nemo audeat vel retinere, vel promovere in ecclesia sibi."—Mansi 3, 883-884.

[5] Gratian says: " Qui vero relicta sua ecclesia ad aliam transire voluerit, nequaquam sine dimissoriis litteris sui episcopi suscipiatur."—C. XXI, q. 2. In C. 1, D. LXXIII Gratian mentions *epistola commendatitia, dimissoria* and *formata.* He tells of the Greek letters used in order to avoid falsification. "Antiqua Christianitas habuit plures ecclesiasticarum litterarum species."—Lupus, *Opera Omnia Canonica,* T. 9, p. 199. Among others Lupus mentions *litterae commendatitiae, pacificae, communicatoriae et formatae.* The definition of *litterae commendatitiae* which he uses makes them identical with *dimissoriae.*

the *litterae dismissoriae* meant permission for a cleric to receive Orders at the hands of a bishop other than his own proper bishop.

Quotations from and reference to the early Councils of the Church will corroborate the first accepted meaning of dimissorial letters in the Church.

Canon 16 of the Council of Nice, 325,[6] says: " Sin autem etiam ausus fuerit quispiam eum, qui ad alium pertinet surripere, et in ecclesia, non consentiente proprio episcopo, a quo recessit qui in canone censetur, irrita fuit ordinatio."

Pope Julius I, 336-352, in a letter to the Oriental bishops said the following under n. 6: " Nullus episcopus alterius praesumat retinere, aut ordinare absque eius episcopi voluntate. . . ."[7]

Canon 13 of the Council of Antioch, 341, expresses the same idea: " Nullus episcopus ex alia provincia audeat ad aliam transgredi ad promotionem aliquos in ecclesiis ordinare, licet consensum videantur praebere nonnulli, nisi literis tam metropolitani quam ceterorum qui cum eo sunt episcoporum rogatus adveniat, et sic ad actionem ordinationis accedat."[8] Likewise canon 19 of the Council of Sardica, 347: "Osius episcopus dixit: Et hoc universi constituimus, ut quicumque ex alia parochia voluerit alienum ministrum sine consensu episcopi ipsius et sine voluntate ordinare, non sit rata ordinatio eius."[9]

The concept of dimissorials which obtained up to the twelfth century was emphasized in the Councils of the times.[10] The

[6] Mansi 2, 675; Hefele 1, 420; c. 3, D. LXXI; c. 23, C. VII, q. 1.

[7] Mansi 2, 1185.

[8] Mansi 2, 1323; Hefele 1, 517.

[9] Mansi 3, 29-30.

[10] Canon 20 of the Council of Chalcedon, 451,—Mansi 6, 1228. Canon 10 of the Council of Auvergne, 535,—Mansi 8, 861; Hefele 2, 762. Canon 15 of the Third Council of Orleans, 538,—Mansi 9, 16. Canon 8 of the Council of Braga, 563,—Mansi 9, 778. Canon 17 of the Fifth-Sixth Council of Constantinople (Trulla), 692: "Nullus omnino clericus, in quocumque sit gradu, potestatem habeat sine proprii episcopi scripta dimissoria in alienae ecclesiae catalogum referri."—Mansi 11, 951; Hefele 3, 333; c. 1, C. XXI, q. 2. Laws of Charlemagne, 779, cap. 6,—Mansi 12, 895. Canon 50 of the

twelfth century brought a change in the concept. As has been seen, the Third Council of the Lateran, 1179, brought forth the new title of patrimony for ordination. It became no longer necessary for a cleric to be perpetually ascribed to a church. He could be sent to another church and there receive Orders from the bishops of that church without becoming ascribed to that second church. Dimissorial letters began to be required only for ordination.[11] The cleric was not absolutely dismissed from his church by these letters but merely sent to another bishop for the purpose of receiving Orders. This is the modern conception of dimissorial letters which obtained from the twelfth century to the present day.[12]

The legal form and content of dimissorials which was given to them in the course of centuries will be discussed with greater benefit in the latter part of this study.

Council of Meaux, 845: "Ut presbyteri, vel quilibet clerici, in alterius parochia sine formata non recipiantur, neque retineantur, nec etiam ministrare sinantur."—Mansi 14, 830. Canon 3 of the Council of Ravenna, 997: "Et quamvis antiquitus sit statutum, ut nullus episcoporum alterius clericum sine commendatitiis litteris recipiat aut ecclesiam in alterius dioecesi consecret, aut aliquem promoveat ad sacrum ordinem qui sit alterius dioeceseos vel per acceptam sive promissam pecuniam . . . "—Mansi 19, 220-221; Harduin 6A, 753-754. Canon 12 of the Council of Gerunda, 1074: "Clerici autem alterius regionis non recipiantur sine proprii Pontificis litteris."—Mansi 20, 520; Hefele 5, 128. Canon 7 of the Council of London, 1138: "Clericos a non suis episcopis absque litteris proprii episcopi ordinatos a susceptorum officiis ordinum inhibemus."—Harduin 6B, 1204-1205; Mansi 21, 512; Hefele 5, 437.

[11] Canon 29 of the Council of Milan, 1287,—Mansi 24, 882; Hefele 6, 255. Canon 10 of the Provincial Council of Rouen, 1231: "Prohibemus ne aliquis clericus ab aliquo quam suo episcopo se faciat ordinari nisi super hoc dioecesani sui litteras habuerit speciales vel licentiam."—Mansi 23, 215; Hefele 5, 1007. Caput 14 of the Provincial Council of Fritzlar, 1246,—Mansi 23, 728. First Provincial Council of Cologne, 1536, P. I, Tit. 29: "Prohibemus quoque, ne officiales nostri litteras dimissorias quae vulgo licentiatoria ordinandi vocantur, alicui temere concedant."—Mansi 32, 1221. Rubric II of the Council of Ravenna, 1314,—Mansi 25, 537; Hefele 6, 568. Canon 6 of the Council of Lambeth, 1330,—Mansi 25, 895. Canon 17 of the Council of Avignon, 1455,—Mansi 32, 188.

[12] It is of historical interest to note that the Council of Trent referred to dimissorial letters with the word *reverendae*.—Sess. VII, *de reformatione*, cap. 10.

PART TWO

COMMENTARY

CHAPTER ONE

Proper Bishop of Ordination

The second part of this study concerns itself with the commentary on canons 955-967 (inclusive) of the Code of Canon Law. Commentators, generally, have not given an extensive commentary on this portion of the Code. The principal and more exhaustive commentaries on ordination and dimissorial letters were written before 1918. Those among the recent authors (since the promulgation of the Code) who have commented on the canons under consideration cling closely to the old law and its commentators. They do this mindful of the principles enuntiated in canon 6 of the Code.[1]

The laws laid down in canons 955-967 with regard to the right to ordain and to grant dimissorial letters are for the most part taken from the old law.[2] The Code has materially changed some of the former laws, the greater part, however, of the canons agree in their fundamental concept with the old law. In view of this fact the old law and its commentators must be consulted together with the modern authors in the interpretation of the canons referred to above.[3]

The first canon which is within the compass of this study reads:

Canon 955

§ 1. Unusquisque a proprio Episcopo ordinetur aut cum legitimis ejusdem litteris dimissoriis.

[1] "Canones qui jus vetus ex integro referunt, ex veteris juris auctoritate, atque ideo ex receptis apud probatos auctores interpretationibus sunt aestimandi."—Canon 6, n. 2.

[2] "Jus vetus" refers to the laws effective at the promulgation of the Code.—Neuberger, N. J., *Canon 6 or the Relation of the Codex Juris Canonici to Preceding Legislation*, Washington, 1927, p. 70.

[3] Canon 6, n. 3.

§ 2. Episcopus proprius, justa causa non impeditus, per se ipse suos subditos ordinet; sed subditum orientalis ritus, sine apostolico indulto, licete ordinari non potest.

This canon lays down the general and positive rule that every one should be ordained by his own bishop. The text clearly rests upon the time-honored principle in the Church of non-interference in and limitation of episcopal jurisdiction. Canon 329, § 1 gives a concise statement of the office of a diocesan bishop. "Episcopi sunt Apostolorum successores atque ex divina institutione peculiaribus ecclesiis praeficiuntur quas cum potestate ordinaria regunt sub auctoritate Romani Pontificis." [4] The rights of a diocesan bishop shall not be infringed upon. It was an immutable and fundamental principle of all legislation in the ancient Church that the bishop ordained only his own subjects. It belongs to the nature and interests of ecclesiastical order that the individual bishop be restricted to his own diocese in the exercise of jurisdiction and thereby refrain from any interference in the jurisdiction of another bishop. This principle has always applied to all episcopal jurisdiction but in a special manner has it been operative in relation to the most important act of episcopal jurisdiction, i. e., the act of ordination. The constant repitition of this fundamental principle and the penalties meted out to those who ignored the regulations manifest clearly the solicitude of the Church in this matter.[5]

Unusquisque, means every baptized male, whether cleric or lay, excluding as is evident one already a priest.

A proprio Episcopo: Apart from the exception made in canon 952 [6] the proper bishop (validly consecrated) is the law-

[4] Canon 239, § 1.

[5] Kober, *Die Suspension der Kirchendiener,* Tübingen, 1862, p. 292. It is hardly necessary to state again that the Pope who has supreme jurisdiction can ordain any one, anywhere without dimissorial letters.—C. 20, 21, C. IX, q. 3.

[6] "Nemini licet ordinatum a Romano Pontifice ad altiorem ordinem promoveret sine Sedis Apostolicae facultate."—Canon 952.

ful minister.[7] He may address dimissorial letters to another bishop. Who is the proper bishop of ordinands, diocesan and religious? This question is answered in the canons that follow.[8]

Ordinetur refers to first tonsure, minor and major Orders. Episcopal consecration is not included because canon 953 in the Code makes special provision for it. A decision of the Pontificial Commission for the Authentic Interpretation of the Code, February 17, 1930, indicates that the word *ordinetur* embraces the conferring of first tonsure.[9]

Aut legitimis ejusdem litteris dimisoriis: The first part of the paragraph contains the general norm and the second part gives a juridical exception, i. e., ordination in virtue of dimissorial letters.[10] Both parts combine to confirm expressly the twofold right of every bishop, namely, the right to ordain and the right to issue dimissorial letters. A further treatment of dimissorial letters is referred to the discussion of later canons.

The text of the second paragraph restates the former law almost in its entirety.[11] The Bishop is excused from ordaining his own subjects if a just cause prevents him from doing so. The cause generally mentioned is sickness. There are other just causes which may hinder a bishop from ordaining his subjects. In order to avoid confusion and not to mistake any point at issue these causes will be examined later in the study.

A bishop of the Latin rite cannot lawfully ordain a subject belonging to the Oriental rite without an apostolic indult. The words *licite ordinare non potest* contain an implicit prohibition.

[7] Simenon-Bouuaert, — *Manuale Juris Canonici,* Gandae et Leodii, 1931, II, 161, nn. 186-187.

[8] Canons 956 and 964.

[9] *A. A. S.*, 22 (1930), 195.

[10] Blat, *Commentarium Textus Codicis Canonici,* Romae, 1924, Lib. III, Pars I, p. 363, n. 302.

[11] Council of Trent, Sess. XXIII, *de reformatione,* cap. 3: "Episcopi per semetipsos ordines conferunt. Quod si aegritudine fuerint impediti, subditos suos non aliter, quam iam probatos et examinatos ad alium episcopum ordinandos dimittant."

The prohibition is found in the Decretals of Gregory IX.[12] The Code in its first canon expressly states that its disciplinary laws are obligatory for the Catholic Church of the Latin rite exclusively except in matters which of their nature affect the Catholic Church of the Oriental rite. With an apostolic indult the proper bishop who may be of the Latin rite can lawfully ordain a subject belonging to an Oriental rite.

Canon 956

Episcopus proprius quod attinet ad ordinationem saecularium est tantum episcopus dioecesis in qua promovendus habeat domicilium una cum origine aut simplex domicilium sine origine; sed in hoc altero casu promovendus debet animum in dioecesi perpetuo manendi jurejurando firmare, nisi agatur de promovendo ad ordines clerico qui dioecesi per primam tonsuram jam incardinatus est, vel de promovendo alumno, qui servitio alius dioecesis destinatur ad normam can. 969, § 2, vel de promovendo religioso, de quo in can. 964, n. 4.

The words, *quod attinet ad ordinationem saecularium,* exclude episcopal consecration on account of canon 953. It is quite clear that this canon concerns itself chiefly with the ordination of candidates for the diocesan clergy, whether these candidates be lay men or cleric. The Code distinguishes between diocesan clerics and the regular clerics in the title *De Ordine.* It considers the ordination of regulars in canon 964.

The proper minister for the ordination of seculars is the Ordinary of a diocese, diocese being taken strictly according to canon 215, § 2. The first requirement on the part of the candidate is domicile in the diocese of the bishop referred to in the preceding sentence as the proper minister. Domicile is defined in canon 92, § 1 as a residence (*commoratio*) in any parish or quasi-parish, or at least in a diocese, vicariate apostolic or prefecture apostolic. With this residence must be connected the intention to remain there permanently or the residence must extend over ten complete years. Not only is domicile required

[12] C. 9, X, *de temporibus ordinationum et qualitate ordinandorum,* I, 11.

but domicile with the place of origin in the diocese (*una cum origine*). The place of origin means the place (any place within the diocese) where the father had a domicile or at least quasi-domicile at the time of the person's birth. This also holds for converts. A former interpretation held that the *locus originis* of converts was not the place of their natural birth but that of their spiritual birth, the place where they were baptized. Natural birth in a place is required to give origin, not conception or adoption.[13] Innocent XII gave a clear cut definition of origin in his Bull, *Speculatores,* par. 4: "Ceterum subditus ratione originis is tantum sit, ac esse intelligatur, qui naturaliter ortus est in ea dioecesi, in qua ad ordines promoveri desiderat; dummodo tamen ibi natus non fuerit ex accidenti occasione nimirum itineris, officii, legationis, mercaturae, vel cuiusvis alterius temporalis morae seu supermanentiae ejus patris in illo loco: quo casu nullatenus ejusmodi fortuita nativitas sed vera tantum et naturalis patris origo erit attendenda." [14] In the event of an illegitimate or posthumous birth the domicile or quasi-domicile of the mother determines the place of origin.[15] The place of origin is of importance in candidates for the diocesan clergy, when at the time of ordination a candidate still retains his domicile in the diocese of origin. The candidate, who was born in a diocese in which he has his domicile, has as his proper bishop for ordination the bishop of that diocese. The title of competence for ordination given to bishops by reason of origin and domicile of the candidate obtained before the Code.[16] It must be recalled that in the old law place of origin alone sufficed, as did simple domicile.[17] The motive of the old law is fully retained in this canon,[18] even though in the

[13] Honorante, *Praxis Secretariae Tribunalis*, cap. I, note 9; Many, *De Sacra Ordinatione*, n. 29.

[14] *Fontes*, n. 258.

[15] Canon 90, § 1.

[16] Gasparri, *De Sacra Ordinatione*, n. 806; Wernz, *Jus Decretalium*, II, n. 28; Many, *De Sacra Ordinatione*, n. 28.

[17] C. 3, *de temporibus ordinationum et qualitate ordinandorum*, I, 9 in VI.

[18] Blat, *Commentarium*, Lib. II, Pars I, p. 364.

present legislation the bishop of origin alone is not competent to ordain a candidate who does not retain a domicile in the diocese of origin. Origin alone does not give competence to any bishop for ordination.

An insertion here of cases may help to clarify the idea of domicile with origin in reference to ordination.

a) While the father has a domicile in the diocese of Rochester a son is born *ex accidenti* in the diocese of Buffalo. Later the father comes to Buffalo and establishes a domicile there. Is the bishop of Buffalo the proper bishop for ordination by reason of domicile with origin? The bishop of Buffalo is not the proper bishop in virtue of domicile with origin. The place of origin according to canon 90 is not Buffalo but Rochester.

b) At the moment of the birth of a son at Wichita Titius had a quasi-domicile there. He lived temporarily in a hotel and later on definitely established himself at Wichita. The son is now a candidate for the diocesan clergy of Wichita. Is the bishop of Wichita competent for his ordination by reason of domicile with origin? In this case he is the proper bishop. Canon 90 states that the place of origin means a place where the father had a domicile or a quasi-domicile at the time of the child's birth. At the time of ordination, the two elements, domicile and origin existed together.

c) This case refers partly to the *aut simplex domicilium sine origine* of the canon. Titius had two domiciles when his son was born, the one in the diocese of Concordia, the other in the diocese of Wichita. The son was born in Wichita. Later on he is a candidate for the diocesan clergy. Is either one of the bishops a proper bishop for ordination? By reason of domicile with origin the bishop of Wichita is the proper bishop for ordination. The bishop of Concordia is also the proper bishop by reason of domicile alone provided the candidate takes the oath to remain permanently in the diocese. The law permits a choice as the word *aut* indicates. If Titius or the son no longer had the domicile in the Wichita diocese at the ordination time then the bishop of Wichita could not ordain him because he would be the bishop of origin without domicile. The bishop of Concordia would be the proper bishop, but only by reason of simple domicile. This case could be still more complicated if for instance the son of Titius had been born *ex accidenti* in the diocese of Leavenworth. It is hardly practical to involve this case because a proper bishop can be found by reason of domicile.[19]

The canon further says *aut simplex domicilium sine origine.* Therefore on the day that a candidate has acquired a domicile in a diocese even though that diocese be not his place of origin he has a proper bishop for ordination. The Code adds a condition to this latter norm, i. e., the oath. In considering the simple domicile it may be well to call attention to canon 93, § 1: a minor, that is, one who has not completed his twenty first year shares the domicile of his parents or guardian. He can have no domicile other than that of his parents or guardian. A minor can acquire a quasi-domicile after the years of infancy but canon 956 does not include quasi-domicile. A candidate, not a minor, can certainly acquire a domicile of his own distinct from that of his parents. As a rule this is not done. The ordinand generally returns to the home of his parents when he is not at the seminary and retains their domicile. The seminarian above twenty one years of age can establish his own domicile elsewhere if he so wills. He does establish a domicile the moment he arrives in the new place with the intention of remaining there permanently. A conditional intention is not sufficient. The intention to remain in a diocese for the purpose of ordination seems to be conditional, e. g., "if I shall be ordained" and consequently not sufficient to establish a domicile. Is this intention conditional? It can hardly be called conditional for "assuming the previous agreement of the bishop to accept a seminarian for his diocese, it is no more conditional than any other intention in which there is always a possibility of circumstances arising which may make one change his mind." [20]

[19] Boudinhon, "Le Propre Évêque D'Ordination", *Le Canoniste Contemporain*, 41 (1918), 290-313.

[20] Woywod, *Commentary*, I, 40; Vermeersch-Creusen, *Epitome*, I, n. 183.

The canons on domicile admit both parochial and diocesan domicile. Every parochial domicile is likewise a diocesan domicile, but not every diocesan domicile is a parochial domicile. A diocesan domicile suffices for ordination.

It has been stated above that the bishop of origin alone is no longer the proper bishop. The candidate, as it frequently happens, may have left the diocese where he was born. Either he may have moved from the diocese of his birth with his parents or for some reason he may have permanently left their home (e. g. in case of death of his parents) and established his own domicile in another diocese. The bishop of his diocese of origin thereby lost all right to ordain him. If the candidate has a domicile in another diocese the bishop of such diocese becomes his proper bishop for ordination. The candidate has a simple domicile. Canon 956 states that in this event the candidate must declare upon oath his intention to remain permanently in the diocese.

The prescription of the oath in the event that the candidate has only a simple domicile, whether legal or acquired, is taken from the Constitution of Innocent XII, *Speculatores*.[21] The Constitution says: "Et nihilominus . . . [promovendus] se vere et realiter animum huiusmodi [perpetuo ibidem permanendi] habere iureiurando affirmet." Canon 956 says: "promovendus debet animum in dioecesi perpetuo manendi iureiurando firmare." The oath of the Code is the same and has the same objective as that required by the Constitution. This oath differs entirely, however, from the oath required in canon 981. It is clear that the candidate who presents himself for tonsure by reason of domicile with origin does not have to take the oath. It appears as quite evident that the object of the oath is to place the candidate into the same condition as the candidate is who presents himself for ordination by reason of domicile with origin. In other words it is a declaration of domicile made under the testimony of an oath. This declaration removes all doubt as to the competence of the bishop of the can-

21 *Fontes*, n. 258.

didate's domicile. It does not permit the candidate to renounce the clause *si nihil inde avocet,* nor does it allow him the strict right to change domicile, since the oath is demanded before the reception of tonsure and the candidate is incardinated by tonsure into the diocese and the possible change of domicile is ordinarily without effect. At the most the candidate will be eligible for excardination.

Blat [22] in his commentary on this canon remarks that the oath binds the candidate for ordination to remain perpetually in the diocese (not parish) for whose service he is promoted, —canon 111, § 2. Such an intention is presupposed because of the simple domicile, however, it is to be confirmed by an oath. The oath may be made into the hands of the bishop himself or of his delegate.[23] This oath causes no difficulty for a candidate who is twenty-one years of age. He is capable of choosing a domicile. The Code does not state the exact age at which tonsure and minor orders may be received but it does say in canon 976 that the candidate for first tonsure must have begun his theological courses. It may happen that a seminarian begins his theological course before he has attained majority. Can he, though a minor, take an oath? He can take the oath for it is not necessary that one be of age in order to take the oath since the text of the canon does not distinguish between major and minor. The minor affirms (just as the candidate who is of age) under oath his intention to remain in the diocese permanently. In a discussion, August 21, 1897, the Sacred Congregation of the Council [24] states that if the *promovendus* is a minor the oath should be taken by his father. This view was held before the Code because of the very strict regulations of the Constitution, *Speculatores,* which were then in force.

The second part of canon 956 deals with three exceptions. In virtue of the discussion which will follow the three exceptional classes are only briefly mentioned here. A more lengthy

[22] Blat, *Commentarium,* Lib. III, Pars I, p. 364.

[23] Augustine, *Commentary,* IV, 423.

[24] *A. K. K. R.,* 79 (1899), 100.

discussion is important since the difficulties which this canon seems to occasion center about the exceptions. One author [25] treats these exceptions with the remark that they are quite obvious and give no canonical difficulties. The first class of exceptions consists of clerics already incardinated into a diocese by first tonsure. Candidates destined for the future service of another diocese according to canon 969, § 2 form the second group of exceptions. Professed religious who are ordained *jure saecularium* belong to the third class.

Boudinhon [26] says that canon 956 has retained the useful elements of the Constitution, *Speculatores,* and has discarded its complications. Blat [27] concludes his commentary on this canon in one sentence. In effect he says that it is therefore clear how to obtain a proper bishop for ordination in the sense of canon 955. The requirements always are: domicile in one's diocese either with origin or with the oath or by incardination whether previous or established with the security of execution. In law, he says, religious profession is equivalent to incardination according to canon 111, § 1.

Even though the legislation contained in canon 956 is quite clear difficulties seem to present themselves in connection with the new discipline. Kinane [28] writing in 1918 remarks "that the most serious of them is that no provision, as far as we can see, has been made for the ordination of those who have no domicile. The result will be that Rome must be approached in each individual case for a remedy. We scarcely believe that it was the intention of the Holy See to leave such a large class unprovided for, and, consequently we think it quite possible that there may have been some error in the drafting of the canon. If the words, *aut simplicem originem sine domicilio,* were substituted for *aut simplex domicilium sine origine,* then

[25] Boudinhon, "Le Propre Évêque D'Ordination", *Le Canoniste Contemporain,* 41 (1918), 308.

[26] *Ibidem, Le Canoniste Contemporain,* 41 (1918), 313.

[27] *Commentarium,* Lib. III, Pars I, p. 365.

[28] Kinane, "The Lawful Bishop for the Ordination of Seculars under the New Code," *I. E. R.,* 11, Fifth Series (1918), 64.

all needs of the situation would be met. In virtue of such a change the bishop of origin would become competent to ordain; and thus provision would be made for all, as nobody can be without a place of origin." The value of this statement is negligible because the writer makes a statement without any proof.

Recently Dr. Schaaf wrote on canon 956.[29] In his article he considered almost all major difficulties in connection with the canon. He does not give a direct answer to the question: "Who is the proper bishop for the ordination of those who have no domicile?" His chief concern is with the difficulty which arises from the fact that incardination no longer seems to make a bishop the proper bishop for ordination.

There are, then, two difficulties at the outset of this discussion. They are contained in two questions. 1) Who is to ordain those who have no domicile? 2) Does incardination alone give one a proper bishop for ordination? In answering these questions an attempt will be made to present both opinions and to point out an apparent incongruity in the new discipline.

The Archbishop of Armagh in a letter dated August 3, 1919 asked the Pontificial Commission for the Authentic Interpretation of the Code: "Who is the proper bishop for the ordination of those who have no domicile?" The reply was private. It said: "As to the question put, the proper bishop is the bishop of the place where the ordination occurs, provided, however, that the person to be ordained acquire a domicile there beforehand with the oath according to canon 956." [30] This reply designates neither the proper bishop nor the domicile for those who have no domicile. The reply does not answer the question otherwise Vermeersch [31] who wrote after the decision had been handed down would certainly not have said that the silence of the Code continues. He suggests an apostolic indult

[29] Schaaf, "Episcopus Proprius Ordinationis", *A. E. R.*, 90 (1934), 352-365.

[30] *Il Monitore Ecclesiastico*, 32 (1920), 57; *Irish Theological Quarterly*, 1919, p. 391; Bouscaren, *The Canon Law Digest*, Milwaukee, 1934, p. 461.

[31] Vermeersch-Creusen, *Epitome*, II, n. 240.

would provide for a proper bishop of ordination. A case may help to present the difficulty more clearly.

Daniel leaves Ireland with the intention never to return to it and thereby he loses his domicile (Canon 95). He comes to the United States. After his arrival here he goes to St. Louis where he decides to enter Kenrick Seminary. His intention is to prepare for service as a priest in the diocese of Cheyenne. The bishop of Cheyenne writes him to the effect that he considers him a student for his diocese. Daniel has nowhere a domicile and consequently he has no proper bishop for ordination. It is impossible for him to establish a domicile in St. Louis for he cannot have the intention to remain there permanently since he is destined for the diocese of Cheyenne. He has not as yet established a domicile in Cheyenne. Daniel is still a layman. The Code does not provide for the excardination and incardination of laymen by letters. A layman is incardinated by first tonsure into a diocese but in order that this may be effected he must have a proper bishop for ordination. Previous to the Code the Holy See issued a Decree [82] by which the excardination and incardination of laymen could be made by an exchange of letters between the excardinating bishop and the incardinating bishop. This mode of transfer was sanctioned by the Holy See because it was not always easy for a young man to establish his own domicile in the diocese for which he wished to be ordained. Even though the Code has made it easier to acquire a domicile it does not provide for the ordination of a candidate who has no domicile.

If Daniel then is unable to establish a domicile let the bishop of Cheyenne, who has accepted him as a student of his diocese, petition the Holy See to designate himself as the proper bishop for the ordination of Daniel. This will be granted by means of an Apostolic Indult.

A case which has some apparent similarity to the above is treated by the Sacred Congregation of the Council, March 10, 1923.[83] In reality it is very different. This case does not

[82] Cong. of the Council, *Decretum*, November 24, 1906,—*Fontes*, n. 4330.

[83] *A. A. S.*, 16 (1924), 51-55.

give anything definite which might pertain to the young man without any domicile.[34]

The question at once presents itself: Has the proper bishop for ordination ever been obtained for those who have no domicile by means of an apostolic indult? Authors since the Code do not cite any instances. Sebastianelli,[35] a pre-code writer, says: " Quod si vagorum vitam sequatur, adeunda est S. Cong. Concilii pro designatione Episcopi quoad ordines eisdem derelictis conferendos."

The discussion of the second difficulty which is concerned with incardination alone may throw some light on the first question.

Some authors [36] hold that a cleric's incardination into a diocese without domicile there does not authorize the bishop of that diocese to ordain him. There are others, notably Capello [37] who seem to hold the opposite view. Eichmann [38] states that incardination makes the incardinating bishop the proper bishop for ordination.

There are two ways in which incardination can take place: 1) By the reception of first tonsure [39] and 2) by formal excardi-

[34] The College of the Propaganda and other seminaries and colleges for the missions which depend upon the S. C. Prop. Fid. still enjoy the rights granted them by the Brief "*Ad Uberes*" of Urban VIII, May 18, 1638,—*A. A. S.*, 13 (1921), 259. The rights they enjoy were mentioned in the historical conspectus of this study.

[35] *Praelectiones Juris Canonici*, Romae, 2 ed., 1905, p. 180.

[36] Maroto, "*De Episcopo proprio quoad ordinationem*", *Apollinaris*, V (1932), 238-245; Kurtscheid, *Das Neue Kirchenrecht*, Paderborn, 2 ed., 1921, p. 13; Biederlack, "Inkardination und Ordination der Saekularkleriker nach dem jetzigen Kirchenrecht", *Zeitschrift fuer Katholische Theologie*, 47 (1923), 50-58; Schaaf, "*Episcopus Proprius Ordinationis,*" *A. E. R.*, 90 (1934), 352-365.

[37] "*Quaestiones canonicae de ordinatione, domicilio et incardinatione,*" *Periodica*, XX (1931), 125-136.

[38] *Lehrbuch des Kirchenrechts auf Grund des Codex Juris Canonici*, Paderborn, 2 ed., 1926, p. 312: "Inkardination eines Klerikers nach erfolgter exkardination (c. 112); der inkardinierende Bischof wird zur Weihe des inkardinierenden Klerikers zustaendig weil er jetzt dessen Herr geworden ist."

[39] Canon 111, § 2.

nation and incardination.[40] The more common way of incardination is through the conferring of tonsure.[41] By means of first tonsure a candidate is promoted to the service of a diocese. Incardination is an inscription to a diocese. After one has been incardinated into a diocese he cannot be incardinated into another diocese unless he has been excardinated from his former diocese.[42] Excardination does not take effect unless incardination into the other diocese follows.[43]

After these brief preliminary remarks on incardination a review of canon 956 will help to establish what connection there is, if any, between incardination alone and the proper bishop for ordination.

The first part of the canon determines the proper bishop for the ordination of diocesan clergy. At first sight it may appear that canon 956 does not distinguish whether the candidate is to receive tonsure, minor or major Orders. This question will be answered in the final summary of the commentary on this canon. If a candidate has been tonsured who is to ordain him to further Orders? Mothon[44] makes the statement that the bishop, "Ordinaire du lieu", can confer minor and major Orders on all clerics already incardinated into his diocese by the admission to tonsure either through himself or through his predecessors.

The second part of the canon deals with the exceptions. The first exception begins with the words *nisi agatur de promovendo ad ordines clerico qui dioecesi per primam tonsuram iam incardinatus est.* They give rise to the opinion that incardination alone makes a bishop competent to ordain the candidate to further Orders. The phrase speaks of a candidate already tonsured. This cleric need not take the oath mentioned in the canon if he remains in the diocese into which he was incardinated by first tonsure. Incardination is equivalent to the oath.

[40] Canon 117.

[41] Vermeersch-Creusen, *Epitome*, I, n. 202.

[42] Canon 112.

[43] Canon 116.

[44] *Institutions Canonique*, Bruges, 1924, II, art. 2046.

In other words domicile with the oath to remain permanently in the diocese and incardination by first tonsure authorize a bishop to ordain a candidate. Can it be said that domicile need not accompany incardination? Has the Code eliminated incardination alone without domicile as a basis for the competence of a bishop to ordain a candidate?

Qui dioecesi per primam tonsuram iam incardinatus est. The word *dioecesi* does not necessarily refer to the bishop of the diocese in which the cleric is incardinated as the ordaining prelate because according to canon 111, § 2 the ordaining prelate may incardinate a subject or a candidate ordained on the strength of dimissorial letters into another diocese.[45] One must keep in mind the stipulation of canon 969, § 2.[46] Some canonists rest their claim on the phrase of the canon quoted above for the opinion that incardination alone gives the bishop authority to promote the candidate to further Orders. Ojetti [47] in his treatise on incardination argues that it is the property of tonsure to incardinate a candidate into a diocese *quasi vi ipsa sua*. Ojetti continues: " Et jure, quia laicus in hypothesi sese offert episcopo, ut operam suam praestet in servitio eius ecclesiae: episcopus eum in hunc finem acceptat et vel tonsuram confert vel alii conferendam committit. Tonsuratus manet ascriptus dioecesi, pro cuius servitio se obtulerat. Quod quidem respondet primaevae Ecclesiae disciplinae, secundum quam 'quilibet episcopus erat proprius pro ordinatione laici, idest poterat laicum cuiuscumque dioecesis ordinare, et ordinatus ita perpetuo ecclesiae ordinantis adscribebatur, ut non posset ad aliam dioecesim transire, aut sine eius licentia ab alio episcopo ad altiores ordines promoveri,' ut dicit Gasparri." [48]

[45] Kurtscheid, *Das Neue Kirchenrecht*, p. 3.

[46] Non prohibetur tamen Episcopus proprius promovere subditum, qui in futurum, praevia legitima excardinatione et incardinatione, servitio alius dioecesis destinetur.

[47] *Commentarium in Codicem Juris Canonici*, Romae, 1930, Lib. II, p. 31.

[48] *De Sacra Ordinatione*, n. 802.

Authors generally bring two replies of the Pontificial Commission for the Authentic Interpretation of the Code into this discussion. One of them has been quoted above. They are both private replies having never been promulgated in the *Acta Apostolicae Sedis.* They are repeated here for the sake of convenience.

1. Quisnam sit Episcopus proprius pro ordinatione illorum qui nullum domicilium habent (c. 956).

2. Utrum ille qui ordinetur a proprio Episcopo servitio alius dioecesis, incardinetur huic alii dioecesi iuxta canonem 111, § 2, an potius dioecesi proprii Episcopi iuxta canonem 969, § 2. Ad. I. Prout dubium exponitur: est Episcopus loci quo fit ordinatio, modo tamen ordinandus praevie acquirat domicilium cum iuramento ad normam canonis 956.

Ad. II. Affirmative ad primam partem; negative ad secundam partem.[49]

It appears that the first question speaks of laymen because a cleric must belong either to some diocese or to some religious community. Under the new discipline it is quite impossible for a cleric to be without a domicile. For, as stated above, once a cleric he is incardinated into a particular diocese, he is ascribed to that diocese permanently. He remains ascribed to it unless he is incardinated elsewhere according to canon 116 or reduced to the lay state. Because of the rules governing formal excardination and incardination a cleric can hardly be without a domicile.[50]

The second question reads: " Whether one who is ordained by his own bishop for the service of another diocese, is incardinated in that other diocese according to canon 111, § 2, or in the diocese of his own bishop according to canon 969, § 2? " The answer says: " In the affirmative to the first part; in the negative to the second." Even though this and the foregoing reply have not been published in the *Acta Apostolicae Sedis* authors recognize them as merely declarative interpretations and therefore need no promulgation.[51]

[49] *Irish Theological Quarterly* (1919), p. 391.

[50] Simenon-Bouuaert, *Manuale Juris Canonici,* I, n. 268.

[51] Canon 17.

Canon 111, § 2 says that by the reception of first tonsure a cleric is ascribed to, or as it is called incardinated in, the diocese for whose service he was promoted.

Canon 969, § 2 says that the bishop is not forbidden to ordain a subject who is destined for the future service of another diocese. When the time comes for the cleric's transfer to the other diocese formal excardination from the diocese of the proper bishop and the incardination into the diocese of another bishop must take place. This canon speaks of clerics.[52] Canon 111, § 2 is concerned only with laymen who are candidates for tonsure and through tonsure become incardinated into a diocese. If a candidate is tonsured according to canon 111, § 2 and promoted for the service of another diocese he is immediately incardinated into that other diocese [53] the two bishops having made a previous agreement to that effect. It must be kept in mind that this candidate was not ordained according to canon 969, § 2. A candidate who is ordained according to canon 969, § 2 is destined for the future service of another diocese. He remains incardinated in his own diocese and retains the bishop who was his proper bishop at the reception of first tonsure. As the canon states his transfer takes place later by means of formal excardination and incardination. The other candidate ordained according to canon 111, § 2 independent of canon 969 does not stand in need of formal excardination and incardination because he was immediately incardinated into the diocese for whose service he was promoted. Does he have to take the oath spoken of in canon 956? If the candidate is being ordained by the proper bishop because of his domicile with origin he need not take the oath. If the candidate has only simple domicile he must take the oath to remain permanently in the diocese into which he is incardinated by first tonsure. Does this incardination by first tonsure into another diocese authorize the bishop of the diocese into which the candidate is incardinated to ordain the cleric to further Orders? Among

[52] Ojetti, *Commentarium*, Lib. II, p. 31, footnote 9.

[53] Vermeersch-Creusen, *Epitome*, II, p. 142, footnote 2; *Nouvelle Revue Theologique*, 47 (1920), 372-373; Vermeersch-Creusen, *Epitome*, I, n. 203.

recent commentators of the Code some definitely hold a negative view.[54] They maintain that a candidate who is incardinated by first tonsure into a second diocese for whose service he was promoted according to canon 111, § 2 must be ordained to further Orders not by the bishop of the diocese for which he was tonsured but by the bishop of the first diocese, i. e., where he has his domicile. Maroto and Schaaf, holding this view, have written at length and specifically answered the question. Their view is couched in the words of Maroto:

"Quod autem in superioribus numeris tradidimus de collatione primae tonsurae, idem tenendum est de subsequentibus ordinationibus usque ad Presbyteratum, si alumnus, servitio alius Dioecesis destinatus, pergit manere in veteri proprio domicilio, idque etiamsi per primam tonsuram fuerit interim Dioecesi destinationis incardinatus; quoniam incardinatio ex se non inducit novi domicilii acquisitionem in Dioecesi incardinationis. Remanet proinde unum domicilium veteris Dioecesi A., ac inde unus eius Episcopus est proprius Episcopus ordinationis pro nostri Aloisii casu; Episcopus autem destinationis vel etiam incardinationis nullum adhuc obtinuit ius ad alumnum, de quo agitur, ordinandum vel ei dandas litteras dimissorias, etenim semper verum est ut in vigenti disciplina nemo potest nisi ex domicilio obtinere Episcopum proprium ordinationis ad normam can. 956. Olim profecto incardinatio, praesertim post decretum S. C. Concilii *A primis* 20 iulii 1898 tribuebat Episcopo incardinanti ius promovendi ad ordines alumnum suae Dioecesi incardinatum, licet nondum in Dioecesi commorantem, ita ut ex titulo incardinationis Episcopus fieret proprius ordinationis eodem iure ac alii erant Episcopi ordinationis proprii ex titulis originis, domicilii, beneficii et familiaritatis: immo aliud eiusdem S. C. Concilii decretum 24 nov. 1906 extendit etiam ad laicos normas excardinationis formaliter faciendae (per litteras proprii Episcopi dimittentis) et incardinationis formaliter faciendae (per litteras Episcopi recipientis), sic

[54] Maroto, "*De Episcopo proprio quoad ordinationem*", *Apollinaris*, V (1932), 238-245; Schaaf, "*Episcopus Proprius Ordinationis*", *A. E. R.*, 90 (1934), 352-365.

nimirum ut etiam laicus fieret incardinantis. Sed haec omnia per novum Codicem antiquata sunt, et ideo laicus est incapax incardinationis, et ipse clericus per solam incardinationem non nanciscitur Episcopum proprium ordinationis, sed dumtaxat per domicilium."

Capello [55] and Eichmann [56] seem to give an affirmative answer to the question. In their opinion the right to ordain belongs to the bishop of the diocese in which the cleric is incardinated, whether he was incardinated by first tonsure or by formal excardination and incardination. Accordingly the candidate who is incardinated according to canon 111, § 2 into a second diocese receives at once the bishop of the second diocese as his proper bishop for further Orders. Capello argues that according to the Code a cleric can be incardinated only in one diocese and have only one proper bishop for ordination. It may be well to quote the text in which this argument is contained. 6. Per incardinationem clericus *propriam* dioecesim ac *proprium* Episcopum sortitur, ut liquet ex dictis. Idcirco laicus qui recipit primam tonsuram servitio alius dioecesis, huic plane incorporatur, ita ut ipsa *propria* fiat eiusque Episcopus *proprium* sit.

Iuxta disciplinam Codicis, clericus *uni* tantum dioecesi potest esse incardinatus et *unum* dumtaxat habere Episcopum *proprium* quoad ordines recipiendos. Quare ea dioecesis, in qua laicus recipit primam tonsuram pro servitio alius dioecesis, ipsi aliena juridice est, et Episcopus ordinans nec est nec manet proprius. Posito facto incardinationis determinatae dioecesis, necessario consequitur eum illius Episcopum fieri proprium, ac propterea ius habere promovendi clericum incardinatum seu subditum suum. Episcopus autem, qui primam tonsuram contulit laico promoto servitio alius dioecesis, eatenus potest altiores ordines eidem conferre, quatenus licentiam seu litteras dimissorias habeat Episcopi proprii ordinandi, seu Episcopi illius dioecesis cui, receptione tonsurae, clericus incardinatus fuit.

[55] "*Quaestiones de ordinatione, domicilio et incardinatione*", *Periodica*, XX (1931), 125-136.

[56] *Lehrbuch des Kirchenrechts*, p. 312.

Itaque, attento responso Pontificiae Commissionis Codicis diei 17 Aug. 1919, genuino sensu atque valore perpenso canonum 111, § 2, 956 et 969, § 2 dicendum ad casum propositum quod attinet, Episcopum B. posse ordinare clericum, tamquam proprium, aut ei dare litteras dimissorias.

If incardination by first tonsure incardinates a candidate into another diocese making the bishop of that second diocese his proper bishop for further Orders it can *a pari* be held that formal excardination of a cleric from one diocese and formal incardination into a second diocese authorize the bishop of the second diocese to confer upon the cleric any further Orders he may stand in need of. It may happen that a candidate ordained according to canon 969, § 2 will not have received all Orders before he is actually incardinated into the diocese for whose future service he was destined.

From the text quoted above Capello, since he makes no mention of the necessity of domicile with regard to simple incardination in the case proposed, one gets the impression that incardination without domicile gives a candidate a proper bishop for ordination. In a later article [57] he emphatically denies that he ever proposed such an opinion.

> " En ipsissima verba a nobis adhibita: 'Ad normam can. 956 Episcopus efficitur proprius quoad ordinationem ex duplici titulo: 1. ratione domicilii una cum origine, quatenus ordinandus habeat tum originem tum domicilium in dioecesi Episcopi ordinantis; 2. ratione domicilii sine origine, praestito tamen jurejurando, quatenus ordinandus animum in dioecesi perpetuo manendi juramento confirmet. Hoc juramentum non requiritur, si agatur a) de clerico ad ordines promovendo, qui per primam tonsuram dioecesi iam incardinatus sit; vel b) de promovendo alumno, qui servitio alius dioecesis sit destinatus; vel c) de promovendo religioso.'
>
> Igitur, secundum doctrinam a nobis traditam, Episcopus ad normam can. 956 est proprius quoad sacram ordinationem ex duplici tantum titulo, nempe vel ratione domicilii cum

[57] "*De Episcopo proprio quoad ordinationem*",—*Periodica*, XXIII (1934), 133-135, 185-190.

origine, vel ratione domicilii sine origine. Ne verbum quidem de tertio quodam titulo, scil. de titulo incardinationis." [58]

Capello's articles apparently offer the following commentary on can. 956: 1) A bishop is a proper bishop for ordination either *ex ratione domicilii cum origine* or *ex ratione domicilii sine origine.* 2) After incardination a cleric can have only one proper bishop for further Orders, i. e., the bishop of the diocese in which the cleric is incardinated. 3) Capello in his article [59] seems to take for granted that every candidate incardinated into a diocese has domicile there. Because of this he cannot be said to hold that incardination alone gives a candidate for Orders a proper bishop.

Previous to the Code two decrees [60] of the Sacred Congregation of the Council regulated the matter of incardination. Of these decrees Chelodi [61] says: "Ex his decretis, quae immediate ad competentiam ordinationis referebantur, normae nunc in C. generaliter pro adscriptione dioecesi translatae sunt, sed formalis incardinatio laicorum praetermissa." In canon 956 the Code does not state that incardination alone without domicile gives one a proper bishop for ordination.

One can be incardinated in two ways, by first tonsure or by formal excardination and incardination. The latter deals with clerics only and therefore presupposes prior ascription to some diocese or religious community. Incardination by first tonsure can only be brought about by one's proper bishop of domicile with origin or of domicile with the oath to remain permanently in the diocese. If the cleric retains his domicile (even though incardinated in another diocese) he is subject to the bishop of his domicile in the same manner as the other faithful. The cleric is subject to the bishop of the diocese in

[58] Capello, "*De Episcopo proprio quoad ordinationem*",—*Periodica*, XXIII (1934), 134.

[59] *Periodica*, XXIII (1934), 185.

[60] *A Primis*, July 20, 1898,—*Fontes*, n. 4307; *Decretum*, November 20, 1906,—*Fontes*, n. 4330.

[61] *Jus de Personis*, n. 106.

which he is incardinated in the special manner of all diocesan clerics. If he is to receive further Orders is the bishop of the diocese of incardination the only one competent to ordain him?

One cannot give an affirmative answer on the strength of canon 956. This canon is silent with regard to incardination as a title of competence for ordination. The old law, as stated in the historical conspectus, gave competence to the bishop of the diocese in which the candidate was incardinated. The new law does not contain the prescription with regard to incardination found in the *A Primis.* The silence of the Code is deliberate,—but is it altogether congruous and consistent? An attempt will be made in the following pages to show that there appears to exist an inconsistency in the present law because of an infringement upon the right of a bishop. Canonical norms of the Code on incardination will form the basis of the following exposition.

The Code is very positive on ascription of clerics to a definite diocese for the service of which the candidate is promoted. This ascription is incardination. An incardinated cleric is under the jurisdiction of the bishop in whose diocese he is incardinated by reason of incardination. If the bishop of that diocese cannot ordain him to further Orders, if that bishop is not the proper bishop for ordination to the exclusion of all other bishops (excepting the right granted by means of dimissorial letters) then his jurisdiction seems to be frustrated. It seems incongruous that the bishop of the diocese in which the cleric is not incardinated should be the one to ordain him, whereas the bishop of the diocese where he is incardinated has no right to confer Orders on him. Canon 969 cannot be invoked in order to remove this incongruity because according to this canon the bishop ordains a subject who is destined for the future service of another diocese but immediately incardinates him into his own diocese and not into the other diocese. Later on when the subject is to be transferred to a second diocese the formal excardination from the diocese of the proper bishop and the incardination into the second diocese must take place. As stated elsewhere the Code does not specify how one is to be destined for future service of another diocese. It is well to note again that canon 969, § 2 says *qui in futurum, praevia legitima excardinatione et incardinatione, servitio alius dioecesis destinetur,* and canon 111, § 2 reads *per receptionem primae tonsurae clericus adscribitur seu, ut aiunt, incardinatur dioecesi pro cuius servitio promotus fuit.*

These two canons cannot be invoked indiscriminately in solving the problems of a proper bishop for ordination and of incardination. Canon 969, § 1 does not refer to the bishop of the second diocese in which a candidate is incardinated by canon 111, § 2. The Code in canon 969 says nothing about any arrangement between the two bishops previous to the ordination of the subject. Therefore it cannot be said that according to canon 969, § 1 the bishop of the second diocese sanctions the ordination of a cleric destined for the future service of a second diocese. The bishop of the second diocese does nothing until the time of transfer of the cleric from his proper diocese to the second diocese.

It must be remembered that according to canon 111, § 2 the ordinand is immediately incardinated into the diocese for whose service he was promoted; that diocese may be his own diocese of domicile or another. Whereas the ordinand of canon 969, § 2 (though destined for the future service of another diocese) is incardinated into his own diocese, i. e., the diocese where the candidate before tonsure had domicile with origin or simple domicile. In order that he may serve another diocese he must be excardinated according to Canon 117. The transfer spoken of in canon 969, § 2 cannot be effected until the candidate has at least received tonsure. It might be advisable that the bishop make some definite arrangement for his subject whom he ordains for the future service of another diocese. A previous arrangement must obtain between the proper bishop of a candidate and the bishop of the diocese into which the candidate is incardinated by first tonsure.

The following case may help to clarify the exposition of the apparent inconsistency in the law.

A layman is ordained by his proper bishop of diocese A according to Canon 111, § 2. At the moment of the reception of tonsure he is incardinated into diocese B for whose service he was promoted. The bishops of diocese A and diocese B had come to an agreement on the candidate previous to the conferring of tonsure. The candidate lost his domicile in diocese A before he had received any further Orders and he has not acquired a domicile in diocese B. Who is to confer further Orders upon this cleric incardinated in diocese B? Can the bishop of diocese B issue dimissorial letters for his ordination by another bishop?

The candidate belongs to diocese B by incardination alone. It does not seem to be in harmony with ecclesiastical legislation on ascription to a diocese that this candidate go to a third diocese, i. e., diocese C and there establish a domicile in order to be ordained for the third diocese. The law has always considered such a candidate a *clericus alienus*. What would happen to his incardination in diocese B? If domicile gives the candidate a proper bishop then in virtue of the fact that he establishes a domicile in diocese C he would have a proper bishop for ordination, and yet he cannot have the intention to remain perpetually in diocese C if he is to be ordained for diocese B. On the other hand it can be assumed that the candidate has decided to remain permanently in diocese C. He wishes to be ordained for that diocese and the bishop of diocese C is willing to accept him. The candidate, however, is a cleric and as such is incardinated in diocese B. The bishop of diocese B may be ready to comply with the cleric's wishes. If so, then formal excardination and incardination must take place. In order to be able to excardinate this cleric the bishop of diocese B must be his proper bishop; for only a cleric's proper bishop can excardinate a cleric.[62] It cannot be denied that the bishop of diocese B is competent to excardinate the cleric in this case. If such is the competency of the bishop of diocese B because of incardination alone it seems that this same bishop

[62] Canon 112.

ought to be competent to ordain the cleric in virtue of incardination.

Neither the declaration of the Pontifical Commission [63] nor the *resolutio* of the Sacred Congregation of the Council, March 10, 1923 [64] can be cited in order to remove the apparent incongruity. Authors [65] indicate that it does not solve the doubt proposed to the Commission. The Irish Theological Quarterly calls the reply a *lapsus memoriae.* Again others merely repeat the answer of the Commission paraphrasing the words of the reply without any further interpretation.[66] Maroto, Capello, Vermeersch and others who commented on the proper bishop for ordination could hardly have lost sight of the particular reply (Ad 1) and its value to the present study if it was of special value.

Bouscaren [67] gives a summary of the *resolutio* mentioned above. It reads: "*Facts.* Joseph, born in diocese N outside of Italy, left it at the age of 15 and went to Italy with his parents. Later he joined the Italian army. After leaving the army, in 1917, he obtained from the bishop of N a letter permitting him to be received as a cleric and ordained by any bishop. He entered a seminary in the town of Y, and, upon asking the S. C. Consist. for permission to be ordained, received the answer: 'Find a bishop who is willing to receive you.' Whereupon, Joseph received tonsure, and later sacred Orders including the priesthood from the bishop of Y upon dismissorial letters from the bishop of X, a diocese which was served by the regional seminary at Y. Thereafter Joseph was always regarded as belonging to the diocese of X, although he never lived there. Disagreement having arisen between Joseph and the bishop of X, Joseph now claims that he belongs to the

[63] *Irish Theological Quarterly* (1919), p. 391, Resp. Ad I.

[64] *A. A. S.*, 16 (1924), 51-55.

[65] Bouuaert-Simenon, *Manuale Juris Canonici,* II, n. 187.

[66] Chelodi, *Jus de Personis,* p. 186, footnote 3; Augustine, *Commentary,* IV, p. 424; *Il Monitore Ecclesiastico,* 32, 57-58; *Nouvelle Revue Theologique,* 47 (1920), 372.

[67] *The Canon Law Digest,* pp. 89-92.

diocese of his origin, N; and in support of the claim makes the following argument:

Argument. The letter of the bishop of N was given in 1917 before the Code. At that time by virtue of a decree of the S. C. Conc., 24 Nov. 1906, excardination of lay persons was permitted, but was required to be in favor of a particular diocese. Since the letter of the bishop of N does not conform to this condition, it must be regarded not as an excardination, but as a simple dimissorial letter, authorizing any other bishop to confer the tonsure and Orders upon Joseph for the diocese of N; which was done. Against the above argument, the following reasons were adduced:

1. It is clear from the very decree of S. C. Conc., 24 Nov. 1906, that the excardination and incardination of lay persons were unknown in the old law. The practice had grown up, it is true, but this so-called excardination was a condition affecting only the licitness and never the validity, of incardination by another bishop.

2. The Code, which became effective before the reception of tonsure by Joseph, entirely does away with the necessity of excardination of lay persons, even as regards licitness. Now, Joseph had lost his domicile of origin at N, and had acquired no new domicile. Hence he was a *vagus*. Since Bishop X was willing to take him, and since he in fact received tonsure upon the latter's dimissorial letters (cf. c. 955), the conditions required by canon 111, § 2 were fulfilled, and Joseph was incardinated in diocese X. The fact that he had no domicile there would at most argue that c. 956 was violated; but it would not in any case make the incardination invalid. Hence:

Question. Does Joseph belong to diocese X in Italy, or to diocese N outside of Italy?

Reply. In the affirmative to the first part; in the negative to the second part."

After a more extensive review of this case as presented in the *Acta Apostolicae Sedis* [68] one fails to find any definite

[68] *A. A. S.*, 16 (1924), 51-55.

statement that incardination alone authorizes a bishop to promate a cleric to further Orders. The document calls attention to the fact that in this case the candidate did not seem to be wanting a domicile because he attended a regional seminary but by a fiction of law Joseph had a domicile in the diocese for which he was studying.

Regional or strictly inter-diocesan seminaries are established in order to supply a diocesan seminary for individual dioceses where there is no diocesan seminary.[69] Seminarians who study in a regional or inter-diocesan seminary for any one of the dioceses which the seminary serves acquire a domicile in the diocese for which they are studying. The bishop for whose diocese they are destined is competent to ordain them or issue dimissorial letters. The document goes on to say that this argument rests on an analogy with the legislation for public cemeteries. Every parish, the Code says, should have its own cemetery unless the local Ordinary has legitimately designated one common cemetery for several parishes.[70] Canon 1354, § 3 provides that an inter-diocesan or provincial seminary may be established with the authority of the Holy See where a diocesan seminary cannot be erected.

Another remark found in the argumentation of the case may be worthy of note: "Nec etiam obstat quod domicilium in eadem dioecesi X tunc non habuerit: hinc etiam *ad summum*—praescindendo a responso S. C. Consistorialis—id arguere liceret, Episcopum in casu contra praescriptum can. 956 egisse: unde certe non sequitur tonsuram invalide collata fuisse." [71] A few lines below the following significant statement is added: "Quod apprime congruit primaevae Ecclesiae disciplinae, vi cuius, teste Emo. Gasparri, *de sacra Ordinat.*, II, n. 802." The quotation from Gasparri is found on a preceding page.

There is no formal excardination and incardination of laymen in the Code.[72] Lay persons are incardinated by first ton-

69 Canon 1354, § 3.

70 Canon 1208, § 1.

71 *A. A. S.*, 16 (1924), 54.

72 Bouuaert-Simenon still think that this method exists.—*Manuale Juris Canonici*, n. 259.

sure. They are to be tonsured by their proper bishop or in virtue of dimissorials.[73] The reception of tonsure gives to the candidate a twofold juridical status. He is received into the clerical state and ascribed to a diocese. This latter juridical status brings with it for every cleric a proper bishop.[74] The Code says that the cleric is ascribed to the diocese for whose service he was promoted.[75] It is on this ascription to one diocese that the main argument for the inconsistency in the law is based. It has been stated above that the ascription by first tonsure to a diocese gives the incardinated cleric a juridical status.[76] Because of this status there seems to be vested in the bishop of the diocese where the cleric is incardinated some jurisdiction over this cleric even though he has no domicile in his diocese. Some proffer the opinion that this title of ordination was of more recent origin than the other titles of competency. One must note that the title of incardination legitimitized in the decree *A Primis* treats solely of formal excardination and formal incardination. "Quae incardinatio clerici ex decreto S. C. C., 20 jul., 1898 supponit excardinationem ex alia dioecesi." [77] The decree does not speak of incardination by first tonsure. Therefore the title of incardination in this decree should properly be called the title of second incardination. This decree was issued to make it lawful for a cleric to be excardinated from the diocese to which he was ascribed. Excardination was not effected until incardination took place. Through the incardination the incardinating bishop received the right to confer further Orders on the cleric. The old concept of ascription was never lost sight of in this decree for ascription in the ancient Church was the chief title of compet-

[73] *A. A. S.*, 22 (1930), 195; Canon 955, § 1.

[74] "Man nennt letzere Rechtsfolge Inkardination (incardinatio, c. 111, § 2). Damit gewinnt der betreffende Tonsurist als Geistlicher seinen *episcopus proprius*."—Koeniger, *Katholiches Kirchenrecht*, p. 139; cf. Noldin, *De Sacramentis*, Editio XIX, Oeniponte, 1929, n. 464.

[75] Canon 111, § 2.

[76] Chelodi, *Jus de Personis*, n. 106.

[77] Wernz, *Jus Decretalium*, II, n. 28.

ency of the proper bishop for ordination. Once this ascription was effected the bishop could promote the cleric so ascribed to higher Orders. It was generally, however, accompanied with domicile. Even though many abuses crept in this concept of ascription has never been changed except for this one factor, i. e., in the early Church ascription meant ascription to a particular church, later it meant ascription to a diocese. The ancient discipline of ascription to a certain definite church remained in force until the promulgation of the Code. It is true a contrary custom had long existed. It was because of the custom which had grown up that the Code introduced incardination or ascription to an entire diocese instead of to a single church of a diocese.[78] The Code [79] expressly states that a cleric is incardinated for the service of a diocese, whether he be incardinated by first tonsure or formally excardinated and incardinated.[80] The new discipline preserves intact the discipline of ascription which obtained since the early days of the Church.[81] Number 4 of the Decree *A Primis* indicated quite clearly that ascription brought with it the right to confer Orders upon the *adscripti*. It, therefore, adds the admonition which obtains today: "Cum tamen nemini sint cito manus imponendae, officii sui noverint esse Episcopi, in singulis casibus perpendere, an, omnibus attentis, clericus adscriptus talis sit, qui tuto possit absque ulteriori experimento ordinari, an potius oporteat eum diutius probari." [82] The Code did not change the concept of ascription in its legislation on incardination. "Die

[78] Canon 111.

[79] Canon 111, § 2.

[80] Canon 117, § 3.

[81] "Reapse disciplina in Ecclesia ea semper fuit, ut clericus per S. Ordinationem clero alicui Ecclesiae inscriberetur stabiliter, cum fieret huius corporis membrum actuosum et pene necessarium. . . . At clericus vi ordinationis, quia alicui Ecclesiae in perpetuum addicebatur, inde firmiter sortiebatur proprium clerum et proprium Prelatum magis firmiter quam si in Dioecesi ordinantis habuisset originem aut domicilium."—*A. K. K. R.*, 79 (1899), 96.

[82] *Fontes*, n. 4307.

Inkardination ist weder ihrem Begriffe noch dem Ausdrucke nach etwas Neues im Kirchenrechte." [83]

Since the Code adheres so closely to the old law with regard to ascription or incardination it does not seem consistent that it depart from one important norm of the old discipline which has always been of the very nature of ascription, i. e. competency for ordination.

It appears more consistent to give the following interpretation of canon 956.

1. The proper bishop for the ordination of candidates for the diocesan clergy is: a) The bishop of the diocese where the candidate (layman) has his domicile with place of origin. If the candidate is ascribed to the diocese of his proper bishop at his initiation into the clerical state this bishop is his proper bishop for further Orders, unless the cleric be excardinated and formally incardinated into another diocese. If the candidate, however, is immediately promoted for the service of another diocese at the reception of first tonsure he is incardinated into the second diocese. The bishop of the second diocese becomes his proper bishop for further Orders. b) The bishop of the diocese where a candidate (layman) has a simple domicile with the oath to remain perpetually in the diocese of simple domicile is also a proper bishop for ordination. A candidate thus promoted to the clerical state is incardinated into the diocese of simple domicile. The bishop of this diocese is competent to confer all other Orders upon the cleric, unless the cleric be excardinated and formally incardinated into another diocese.

2. The canon gives three classes of exceptions. a) To the first class belong clerics who have already been incardinated by first tonsure into a diocese. They have their proper bishop in virtue of ascription to a diocese.[84] b) To the second class belong candidates (laymen) who are subject to a bishop by domicile alone and are destined for the future service of another

[83] Biederlack, "Inkardination und Ordination der Saekular-Kleriker nach dem jetzigen Kirchenrecht," *Zeitschrift fuer Katholische Theologie*, 47 (1923), 50.

[84] *Jus Pontificium*, 3 (1923), 8.

diocese. They are not required to take the oath to remain permanently in the diocese of their domicile for they do not intend to remain there.[85] Neither, as is evident, is it required that the place of origin be in the same place of domicile. They are incardinated into the diocese of the bishop where they have their domicile. He is their proper bishop for further Orders until the excardination and incardination are effected.[86] c) To the last class of exceptions belong the professed religious whose ordination is governed by the law for the ordination of the diocesan clergy. The proper bishop of these candidates will be more fully determined in the commentary on canon 964, n. 4.

Every candidate for ascription or incardination into a diocese must have a domicile in the place of origin, or a domicile with the oath to remain in that diocese permanently in order to have a proper bishop for ordination. After his incardination into a diocese the bishop of the diocese where the cleric is incardinated is his proper bishop for further Orders. A cleric, therefore, has one proper bishop, i. e., the bishop of the diocese where he is incardinated. A candidate for incardination (a layman) may have two proper bishops for ordination, i. e. the bishop of his domicile in the place of origin, and the bishop of simple domicile joined to the oath to remain permanently in the diocese.

In presenting this interpretation of canon 956 as seemingly more consistent one must remember that the Code does not say that incardination alone gives competence for ordination to a bishop. The Code requires domicile in the diocese of the proper bishop of ordination.

Canon 957

§ 1. Vicarius ac Praefectus Apostolicus, Abbas vel Praelatus *nullius*, si charactere episcopali polleant, Episcopo dioecesano aequiparantur quod pertinet ad ordinationem.

§ 2. Si episcopali charactere careant, possunt nihilominus in proprio territorio et durante munere, conferre primam tonsuram et

[85] *A. A. S.*, 16 (1924), 54.

[86] Canons 969, § 2 and 117.

ordines minores tum propriis subditis saecularibus ad normam can. 956, tum aliis qui litteras dimissorias iure requisitas exhibeant; ordinatio extra hos fines ab eisdem peracta irrita est.

This canon is actually a further explanation and confirmation of canon 951. It speaks of ministers who are *per se* extraordinary ministers of ordination. The Code calls some of them inferior prelates.[87] They are prelates but not necessarily bishops. If they are consecrated bishops they are equal to diocesan bishops in the matter of ordination and they are then ordinary ministers of ordination. The Code defines the prelates mentioned in this canon and determines their part in the government of the Church.

The Vicar Apostolic is generally a bishop.[88] He governs a territory which has not been erected into a diocese.[89] The territory, in which he has ordinary vicarious power, is called a vicariate. His power is ordinary because it is by law attached to an office.[90] It is vicarious because he does not exercise power in his own name but in the name of the Roman Pontiff. The Vicar Apostolic is an *ordinarius loci.*[91] His appointment takes place by means of Apostolic Letters.[92] What has been said of the Vicar Apostolic is likewise true of the Prefect Apostolic except that the latter is rarely a bishop,[93] and his appointment is made by means of a decree from the Sacred Congregation of the Propaganda.

Abbots and Prelates *nullius* are defined as prelates who rule over the clergy and people of a territory that is separated from every diocese.[94] Their proper territory is no diocese. In law the word " diocese " refers also to abbeys and prelatures *nullius*

[87] Chapter X, Title VII, Book II of the Code.

[88] Vermeersch-Creusen, *Epitome*, I, n. 364.

[89] Canon 293, § 1.

[90] Canon 197, § 1.

[91] Canon 198, § 1.

[92] Canon 293, § 2.

[93] Vermeersch-Creusen, *Epitome*, I, n. 364.

[94] Canon 293, § 2.

unless the law decrees otherwise.[95] Abbots and prelates *nullius* are canonically instituted or nominated by the Roman Pontiff without prejudice to the right of election or presentation.[96] They are Ordinaries in their proper territory.[97] Generally it can be said that they have the same rights and obligations which belong to residential bishops in their own diocese.[98] A prelate *nullius* is quite frequently a bishop since the prelature is usually intended to become a bishopric. An abbot *nullius* is sometimes a bishop. If an abbot and prelate *nullius* have episcopal consecration they are also equal to a diocesan bishop with regard to ordination.

The second paragraph of canon 957 properly considers the prelates as extraordinary ministers of ordination, i. e., if they are not consecrated bishops. These prelates, if they lack episcopal consecration, may confer tonsure and minor Orders upon their own subjects. They may also ordain to tonsure and minor Orders others, religious or seculars, on the strength of dimissorial letters from their proper religious superiors or from their proper Ordinaries. The word *aliis* does not mean *alienis* otherwise it would have to be interpreted as signifying seculars only. *Aliis* means *non subditi,* seculars or religious.[99]

The limitations of the power of these Ordinaries (when lacking episcopal consecration) constitute the negative portion of canon 957. The first limitation is contained in the words *in territorio proprio et durante munere.* There is no great difficulty in determining the proper territory or district of the individual Ordinary mentioned above for the law is clear. The Code is equally clear in regard to the term of office.[100]

[95] Canon 215, § 2.

[96] Canon 320, § 1. There were 27 abbeys and prelatures *nullius* according to the *Annuario Pontificio,* 1930. An abbey or prelature *nullius* can only be established by the Roman Pontiff. The United States has one Abbey *nullius* at Belmont, N. C.

[97] Canon 198, § 1.

[98] Canon 323, § 1.

[99] Blat, *Commentarium,* Lib. III, Pars I, n. 304.

[100] Cap. VIII, X, Tit. VII, Lib. II.

The canon enjoins a second limitation when it forbids the prelates (if they are not consecrated bishops) to ordain without dimissorial letters those who are not their subjects. It may be asked whether dimissorial letters are required for the valid conferring of tonsure and minor Orders? The common opinion is that dimissorials are necessary for the validity of the ordinations by those who lack episcopal consecration.[101] Augustine says that "the legislator who confers power can make the exercise thereof dependent on the fulfillment of certain conditions." [102]

[101] Woywod, *Commentary*, n. 223, p. 110.

[102] *Commentary*, IV, p. 426.

CHAPTER TWO

DIMISSORIAL LETTERS

THE concept of dimissorial letters in the early Church and their later signification have been indicated in the historical conspectus of this study. It is the purpose of this chapter to present the legislation of the Code on dimissorial letters. Canons 958-963 (inclusive) give the norms for dimissorial letters in the new discipline with regard to the ordination of diocesan clergy,[1] and those ordained *jure saecularium.*[2] The dimissorial letters *pro regularibus* will be treated in the next chapter.

SECTION ONE

The Code does not explicitly define dimissorial letters in the canons under consideration. It speaks of their effect, their necessity,[3] of how, by whom and to whom they should be granted.

Dimissorial letters may be defined as a delegation of the faculty to confer Orders.[4] The granting of dimissorial letters pertains to episcopal jurisdiction rather than to the power of Orders. To issue a dimissorial letter is strictly an act of jurisdiction.[5] Reiffenstuel renders the definition of dimissorial letters in the following words: " Per dimissorias intelliguntur illae litterae, in quibus continentur scripta licentia, et consensus proprii praelati, et eius subditus possit ab alio episcopo ordin-

[1] Canon 956.

[2] Canon 964, n. 4.

[3] Canon 955, § 1.

[4] Vecchiotti, *Institutiones Canonicae,* Editio decimanona, Augustae Taurinorum, 1886, p. 35.

[5] " Der Rechtsgrund fuer deren (dimissoriales) Ausstellung ist die Jurisdiktion."—Koeniger, *Katholisches Kirchenrecht,* p. 143; Hinschius, *System,* I, p. 94.

ari."[6] Many[7] gives the concept of dimissorial letters as "*potestas ab auctoritate competenti concessa alicui episcopo, ordinandi non propium subditum.*" The correlative of this is "*licentia ab auctoritate competenti concessa subdito, recipiendi ordinem ab episcopo non proprio.*" This study cannot and need not concern itself in detail with any other letters required for ordination even though mention is made of the testimonial letters. Among the later pre-Code writers Wernz gives a very adequate definition of dimissorial letters: "*Dimissoriae dicuntur litterae quibus proprius ordinandi Praelatus vi suae jurisdictionis rogat vel deputat Episcopum sive specialiter sive generaliter determinatum, ut subdito suo, de cuius idoneitate simul authenticum dat testimonium, ordines conferrat.*"[8] The above definitions are valid and quite adequate even though they are given by authors who wrote before the promulgation of the Code. Commentators on the Code generally do not give any definitions of dimissorial letters. They accept the definitions of the pre-Code writers. The definition given by Vermeersch[9] is an example of this: "*Litterae dimissoriae sunt litterae quibus episcopus vel Superior competens subditos suos mittit ad alienum episcopum ut ab hoc ordinetur.*" A proper definition of these letters can readily be formulated from the norms of the new discipline about to be considered. In the Code these dimissorial letters signify the written permission to be ordained by a bishop other than one's own.[10] They are the letters of a proper Ordinary granted *vi suae jurisdictionis* for the ordination of his own subject at the hands of another bishop. They are, as it were, a legal substitute for the proper bishop of ordination. Is it always lawful for the proper bishop of ordination to make use of this substitute? The Code decrees that the proper bishop shall himself ordain his own subjects, *justa causa non impedita* (Canon 955, § 2). The Code prefers the

[6] *Jus Canonicum Universum*, I, XI, n. 109.

[7] *De Sacra Ordinatione*, n. 60.

[8] Wernz, *Jus Decretalium*, II, n. 29.

[9] Vermeersch-Creusen, *Epitome*, II, n. 241.

[10] Perathoner, *Das Kirchliche Gesetzbuch*, Brixen, 1923, p. 274, footnote 1.

ordination by the proper bishop to the granting of dimissorial letters. The Council of Trent clearly expressed this preference.[11] It gave sickness as a just cause which might prevent a bishop from ordaining his own subjects. In specifying sickness as a cause it did so not *taxative* but rather *indicative*, thereby resting the matter on the conscience of every bishop. Other reasonable causes may prevent the proper bishop from ordaining his own subjects, e. g. legitimate absence from his diocese at the time of ordination, or the absence of the candidate from the diocese of his proper bishop. The latter happens when, for instance, a candidate is in Rome for studies and his proper bishop for ordination is in the United States.[12] Almost every commentator refers to the just cause of canon 955, § 2 in the manner of Schmalzgrueber[13] "*aegritudo, vel aliud impedimentum, ob quod episcopus proprius vel nolit, vel nequeat ordinare.*" In other words sickness is given as an example of one of the just causes.[14] Augustine[15] advances the opinion that the Code is more liberal than the Council of Trent and the Constitution of Innocent XIII, *Apostolici Ministerii*, September 23, 1724.[16] He states that the latter mention only one cause, i. e. sickness, which would justify a bishop in not ordaining his own subjects. This opinion cannot be maintained since they do not exclude other reasonable causes. The Code admits any just cause.

Whatever the just cause might be which moves a proper bishop to grant dimissorial letters must it be mentioned in the dimissorial letters? The canons do not expressly answer this question. The Council of Trent determined that the cause should be mentioned in the dimissorials.[17] Reiffenstuel[18]

[11] Sess. XXIII, *de reformatione*, cap. 3; Gasparri, *De Sacra Ordinatione*, n. 877.

[12] Gasparri, *De Sacra Ordinatione*, n. 877.

[13] *Jus Ecclesiasticum*, III, XI, n. 50.

[14] Blat, *Commentarium*, Lib. III, Pars I, n. 302.

[15] *Commentary*, IV, p. 420.

[16] *Fontes*, n. 280.

[17] Sess. IX, *de reformatione*, cap. 2: "*ob quam a propriis episcopis ordinari non possint, in litteris exprimendam.*"

[18] *Jus Canonicum Universum*, I, XI, n. 116.

quotes the above passage from the Tridentine Council and concludes that the cause should appear in the letters. He adds, however, that in some provinces the custom obtained to omit the just cause. Schmalzgrueber [19] likewise refers to the custom. It is also the opinion of Hinschius [20] that the cause be written into the letters. He bases his claim on the *Liber Sextus* of Boniface VIII.[21] This text of the *Liber Sextus* had immediate application to the ordination of the *ultramontani* in Italy. Wernz [22] does not say any more than that the bishop who is prevented *ex aegritudine vel alia legitima causa* from ordaining his own subjects may issue dimissorial letters. Honorànte,[23] on the contrary, states that *dimissoriae non admittuntur etiam pro prima tonsura, in quibus non contineatur causa, ob quam a proprio episcopo ordinari non possint illas obtinentes.*[24]

The conclusion at which one can arrive upon a consideration of the authors' statements may be worded as follows. The just cause which prevents a bishop from ordaining his own subjects *may* but *need not* be mentioned in the dimissorial letters. Wernz, Many, and Gasparri, who are among the more recent pre-Code commentators, do not demand that mention be made of the just cause in the dimissorials. Commentators since the Code do not concern themselves with this question.

Another question might be asked: Is it necessary that the *licentia episcopi proprii ad conferendos ordines suo subdito ab alio episcopo* be given in writing? It is certain that a tacit or presumed permission will not suffice.[25] The consent must be

[19] *Jus Ecclesiasticum*, III, XI, n. 50.

[20] *System*, I, p. 96.

[21] C. 1, *de temporibus ordinationum et qualitate ordinandorum*, I, 9 in VI: "*per eius patentes Litteras causam rationabilem continentes, quare ipsum nolit, aut nequeat ordinare.*"

[22] *Jus Decretalium*, II, n. 29.

[23] *Praxis Secretariae Tribunalis*, 2 ed., Romae, 1762, cap. VI, nota 2, p. 73.

[24] Aichner, *Compendium Juris Ecclesiastici*, 6 ed., Brixinae, 1887, p. 198: "*In litteris dimissoriis ... exprimi opus est ... causam ob quam proprius vel nolit vel nequeat ordinare.*"

[25] Wernz, *Jus Decretalium*, II, n. 29; Gasparri, *De Sacra Ordinatione*, n. 862; Many, *De Sacra Ordinatione*, n. 63; Sess. XIV, *de reformatione*, cap. 2.

the express consent of the proper bishop. It may be given verbally or in writing. Wernz [26] says that *per se et ordinarie* express consent given *viva voce* is sufficient. Many also holds that *jure communi dimissoriales concedi possunt verbo.*[27] He rests his statement on the Council of Trent.[28] The Tridentine Council uses the expression *absque sui praelati proprii expresso consensu aut litteris dimissoriis.* Both authors favor the granting of dimissorials in writing.[29] Many favors this form because it is more satisfactory in helping to avoid deceit and in giving greater certitude to the authenticity of the dimissorials. Wernz states that the permission *ex communiter contingentibus per scriptas litteras concedi solet.* Gasparri [30] agrees with the above authors.

Even though the permission to receive Orders from a bishop other than one's proper bishop need not be granted in writing [31] the more common form of procedure is to issue the letters in writing. This appears from the fact that formularies for dimissorial letters have been drawn up by various authors [32] and from the fact that printed forms are actually used in the diocesan chanceries.

Section Two

Canon 958

§ 1. Litteras dimissorias pro saecularibus dare possunt, quamdiu jurisdictionem in territorio retinent:

1. Episcopus proprius, postquam possessionem suae dioecesis legitime ceperit ad normam can. 334, § 3 licet nondum consecratus;

2. Vicarius Generalis, ex speciali tamen Episcopi mandato;

[26] *Jus Decretalium*, II, n. 29.

[27] *De Sacra Ordinatione*, n. 63.

[28] Sess. XIV, *de reformatione*, cap. 2.

[29] If the consent is given orally it must be given in the presence of the ordaining prelate. Cf. Gasparri, *De Sacra Ordinatione*, n. 862.

[30] *De Sacra Ordinatione*, n. 863.

[31] Reiffenstuel, *Jus Canonicum Universum*, I, XI, n. 110.

[32] Mothon, *Institutions Canoniques*, Bruges, 1924, III, p. 296; Gasparri, *De Sacra Ordinatione*, pp. 319-322; Baart, *Legal Formulary*, 3 ed., New York, 1898, pp. 202-203.

3. De Capituli consensu Vicarius Capitularis post annum a sede vacante; intra annum vero solis arctatis ratione beneficii recepti vel recipiendi, aut ratione certi alicuius officii, cui propter necessitatem dioecesis sine dilatione sit providendum;

4. Vicarius ac Praefectus Apostolicus, Abbas vel Praelatus *nullius* licet episcopali charactere careant, etiam ad ordines maiores.

§ 2. Vicarius Capitularis litteras dimissorias ne concedat eis qui ab Episcopo rejecti fuerunt.

The Code explicitly requires dimissorial letters for the ordination of a candidate by any bishop other than his own proper bishop.[83] They are always necessary when an ordinand is not subject to the ordinary jurisdiction of the ordaining bishop.[84]

Canon 958 specifies who has the power to grant dimissorial letters for the diocesan clergy, and those who are ordained *jure saecularium.* The first words of the canon give a general norm, i. e. *quamdiu jurisdictionem in territorio retinent.* The persons mentioned in numbers 1-4 (inclusive) of paragraph one must have jurisdiction in their proper territory at the time they issue the dimissorial letters. One may distinguish a twofold requirement contained in the words jurisdiction and territory. This recalls a previous statement that the jurisdiction of an Ordinary (excepting the Roman Pontiff) is limited to his own territory. Jurisdiction and territory are very closely linked together so that an Ordinary can hardly retain a territory as his own without at the same time enjoying jurisdiction in that territory. When an Ordinary is given jurisdiction he at the same time receives a territory proper to him wherein he can exercise the jurisdiction. The phrase of the canon does not say that the Ordinary must actually be present (physically) in the territory in order to retain his jurisdiction. It does say that he must have jurisdiction in a definite territory.

Accordingly the first Ordinary mentioned in number one of canon 958, § 1, is the *episcopus proprius.* The proper bishop

[83] Canon 955, § 1.

[84] Pruemmer, *Manuale Juris Canonici,* p. 405.

is the one spoken of in canon 956. Number one of the canon under consideration adds *postquam possessionem suae dioecesis legitime ceperit ad normam can. 334, § 3 licet nondum consecratus.* A bishop-elect who has taken canonical possession of his diocese, even though not yet consecrated, is competent to issue dimissorial letters. When he takes possession of his diocese he at once has jurisdiction in that diocese. The canonical possession is effected through the presentation of the apostolic letters of appointment (either by himself or by a proxy) to the cathedral chapter or diocesan consultors in the presence of the secretary of the chapter or of the diocesan chancellor.[35] The Metropolitan (Archbishop) may issue dimissorial letters before he has received the pallium. He must have the pallium before he can ordain.[36]

Number two of paragraph one gives one of the instances[37] in which the Vicar General cannot act without a special mandate from the bishop. The bishop may give this mandate orally or in writing, for one case or for several cases. An opportunity may present itself when the bishop could give the Vicar General the special mandate, e. g., during the bishop's absence or illness.

In number three of paragraph one the Vicar Capitular or the Administrator (in countries where there are not Cathedral chapters) can also grant dimissorial letters. The Code retricts his power by means of two specific limitations. a) The consent of the Chapter or of the Diocesan Consultors is required. Mere advise of these bodies will not suffice. Any action taken by the Vicar Capitular or Administrator without the consent or contrary to the vote of the Chapter or consultors is invalid.[38] The law expressly states that the consent of the chapter or of the diocesan consultors must be obtained before the Vicar Capitular or Administrator can grant dimissorials. b) The power of the Vicar Capitular or Administrator is further limited by

[35] Canon 334, § 3.

[36] Canon 276; *Ceremoniale Episcoporum*, Lib. I, cap. XVI, n. 6, coll. 863.

[37] Canon 368, § 1.

[38] Canon 105, n. 1.

the element of time. *Post annum,* i. e. he may not exercise his power until a year has elapsed from the day the See became vacant. The time of this vacancy must be computed according to canon 34. In the transfer of a bishop from one See to another the first See becomes vacant when he has taken canonical possession of the second See according to canon 194.

One exception is mentioned in this number in reference to the time limit. The Vicar Capitular or Administrator may issue dismissorials within a year to those who must be ordained. To this class belong candidates who have received or are to receive a benefice. They are called *arctati.* Because of the benefice they have received or are to receive the candidates are considered as forced to obtain some Order, generally a sacred Order within a year. Likewise candidates who have received or are to receive a certain office which on account of the needs of the diocese must be filled without delay are called *arctati.* The deceased bishop may have appointed a cleric to an office requiring the priesthood and this office must be filled within a year.

Both Many and Gasparri hold that candidates for first tonsure can hardly be included among the *arctati* since *prima tonsura non est ordo.*[39] This particular argument can not be advanced under the new discipline since the Code uses the words, "ordain", "order", "ordination", "sacred ordination" in reference to all Orders including first tonsure, unless the text of the law refers to a particular Order. (Canon 950) In Number three the Code does not distinguish between the Orders and first tonsure. It seems that the number three refers to sacred Orders because under the present discipline few clerics in minor Orders hold any benefices. Neither can they ordinarily supply the needs of a diocese. Candidates for first tonsure and minor Orders, therefore, can rarely be classed with the *arctati.* The question whether under the Code any *arctati ratione beneficii* can exist is open to some speculation because of the regulations of the Code with regard to ecclesiastical

[39] Many, *De Sacra Ordinatione*, n. 61; Gasparri, *De Sacra Ordinatione*, n. 869.

benefices. Since, however, canon 958, § 1, n. 3 mentions them one is within the law to accept the possibility of their presence. It may happen that a diocese stands in great need of priests. Augustine [40] cites the instance of France which before the war was short of 3,000 priests.

The words of the canon *certi alicuius officii* refer to a definite ecclesiastical office in the strict sense.[41]

Apart from the provision of *infra annum* the canon does not further specify. It appears that the dimissorial letters for *arctati* may be issued at any time after the See is vacant by the Vicar Capitular or Administrator provided he has the consent of the chapter or of the Consultors. Before the Code the cathedral chapter could issue dimissorial letters prior to the election of a Vicar Capitular.[42] It no longer enjoys this right in the Code.

Number four of canon 958, § 1 is a sequence of canon 957, § 2. It goes one step farther in giving the *Ordinarii* mentioned in both canons the right to grant dimissorials for all major Orders. As far as ordination is concerned these prelates (without episcopal consecration) can only confer first tonsure and minor Orders, but in regard to dimissorial letters they can issue them for all Orders to their subjects. The new law changes the old law. In the old law Prelates and Abbots *nullius* could not grant dimissorial letters to their secular subjects for any Orders.[43] The *episcopus vicinior* had the right to ordain their subjects or issue dimissorials.[44] The bishop whose cathedral church was nearer to the abbatial church or to the church of the prelature *nullius* was considered the *episcopus vicinior*.

The Abbots and Prelates *nullius* mentioned in this canon govern a territory which in law according to canon 215, § 2,

40 *Commentary*, IV, p. 428.

41 Canon 145, § 2; Blat, *Commentarium*, Lib. III, Pars I, n. 305.

42 Many, *De Sacra Ordinatione*, n. 61; Gasparri, *De Sacra Ordinatione*, n. 871; Sess. VII, *de reformatione*, cap. 10.

43 Council of Trent, Sess. XXIII, *de reformatione*, cap. 10.

44 Many, *De Sacra Ordinatione*, n. 61.

is equivalent to a diocese unless the law decrees otherwise. In the event that their government of the *nullius* is impeded provision is made through the Metropolitan of their choice.[45] This choice is made permanently with the approval of the Holy See.[46] A pro-vicar or pro-prefect Apostolic takes the place of the Vicar or Prefect Apostolic if their jurisdiction is impeded according to canon 429, § 3.[47] The Pontifical Commission for the Authentic Interpretation of the Code was asked whether the pro-vicar [48] can grant dimissorials within a year from the vacancy of the See. The Commission, July 20, 1929, ad I, replied in the affirmative.[49] In virtue of this reply the pro-vicars and pro-prefects Apostolic may be included among the Ordinaries enumerated in canon 958, § 1, n. 4. They are deputed *ex jure* to grant dimissorials in conformity with this canon.[50] No mention is made of the Apostolic Administrator in this canon. He rightly belongs among those who can grant dimissorial letters since he enjoys the same rights and has the same duties as the residential bishops,[51] if he is permanently appointed. If his appointment is *ad tempus* [52] he has the rights and duties of a Vicar Capitular or diocesan administrator. The Apostolic Administrator who has episcopal consecration may not only issue dimissorials but he also can ordain all subjects belonging to the diocese of which he is administrator.

The last paragraph of this canon contains a direct prohibition. The Vicar Capitular or Administrator shall not grant dimissorial letters to any one who has been rejected by the bishop. This is a protection of episcopal authority and of the unity of government. This norm is not expressly contained in the former law but can be deduced from the old law

[45] Canon 429, § 5.

[46] Canon 285.

[47] Canon 309, § 2.

[48] Canon 310, § 2.

[49] *A. A. S.*, 21 (1929), 573.

[50] *Jus Pontificium*, 9 (1929), 193.

[51] Canon 315, § 1.

[52] Canon 315, § 2.

which restricts the power of the Vicar Capitular. A similar enactment is found in canon 44 concerning rescripts. Canon 44, § 2 states that a favor refused by the bishop cannot validly be granted by the Vicar General. Blat [53] points out that Vicar Capitular mentioned in canon 327, § 1 is also bound to observe this law. The Vicar Capitular of a diocese and the Vicar Capitular of a *nullius* govern a territory to which the law applies the one term " diocese " unless otherwise specified. It follows then that if an Abbot or Prelate *nullius* has rejected anyone from ordination the Vicar Capitular [54] of the Abbey or prelature *nullius* shall not grant dimissorials to him.

Canon 959

Qui potest litteras dimissorias ad ordines recipiendos dare, potest quoque eosdem ordines conferre per se ipse, si necessarium ordinis potestatem habeat.

Bouix [55] gives a very concise statement on the matter of this canon in the words: " *Extra controversiam est apud doctores.*" This statement is valid today. Whoever has the right to grant dimissorial letters for the reception of Orders may confer these Orders himself, provided he possesses the necessary power of Orders. The granting of dimissorials supposes the power of jurisdiction. All *ordinarii proprii* who have the necessary jurisdiction to issue dimissorial letters to their own subjects can likewise confer the same Orders. In conferring Orders, however, the *ordinarii proprii* must not only have jurisdiction but they must also have the power of Orders. Thus prelates, who lack episcopal consecration, may be competent to grant dimissorial letters but cannot confer the Orders.

Canon 960

§ 1. Litterae dimissoriae ne concedantur, nisi habitis antea omnibus testimoniis, quae iure exiguntur ad normam can. 993-1000.

[53] *Commentarium*, Lib. III, Pars I, n. 305.

[54] Canon 327, § 1.

[55] *Tractatus de Episcopo*, Parisiis, 1859, Tomus II, p. 151.

§ 2. Si post datas ab Ordinario litteras dimissorias nova testimonia necessaria sint ad normam can. 994, § 3, Episcopus alienus ne ordinet, antequam receperit.

§ 3. Quodsi promovendus tempus sufficiens ad contrahendum impedimentum ad normam mem. can. 994 transegerit in ipsa dioecesi Episcopi ordinantis, hic testimonia directe colligat.

This canon connects dimissorial letters with testimonial letters. A lengthy discussion of testimonial letters cannot be taken up here. It suffices to note the references made by canon 960 to testimonial letters.

The testimonial letters may be defined as the letters given by competent authority testifying to the worthiness of an ordinand.[56] They are so closely linked to dimissorial letters because no bishop can send one of his subjects for ordination to another bishop unless he can testify to the candidate's fitness. The Council of Trent decreed: . . . "*quod si aegritudine fuerint impediti, subditos suos, non aliter quam iam probatos et examinatos, ad alium episcopum dimittant.*"[57] The reason for this legislation is quite clear. If no bishop may ordain his own subjects without having proved and examined them it follows that he may not send them to another bishop for ordination without being assured of their fitness. The first paragraph of this canon requires all testimonies to be in the hands of the proper Ordinary before he issues dimissorials. No dimissorial letters shall be issued without the testimonial letters demanded in canons 993-1000.

The importance of testimonial letters is stressed in paragraph two of this canon. Even though dimissorials have been issued the ordaining bishop is not to confer Orders on a candidate who stands in need of new testimonials until he has received these letters. The norm making further testimonial letters necessary is contained in canon 994, § 3. There is a necessity for additional testimonials if the candidate has again lived for

[56] Many, *De Sacra Ordinatione*, n. 121.

[57] Sess. XXIII, *de reformatione*, cap. 3; Sess. XXIII, *de reformatione*, cap. 8.

three months or six months in a diocese before his ordination and since the last testimonial letters were issued. A candidate may have contracted a canonical impediment during a six months' stay in a diocese after the age of puberty. For the men in military service the time limit is three months.[59]

The obligation of obtaining the testimonial letters rests upon the proper Ordinary of the candidate since the first paragraph of canon 960 decrees that dimissorial letters shall not be granted until the testimonials have been received. It is clear from what has gone before that only the proper Ordinary can grant testimonial letters. Paragraph three of this canon makes an exception to the general rule. It states that if the ordinand has lived in the diocese of the ordaining bishop long enough to contract a canonical impediment (i. e. three months for men in military service and six months for others) the ordaining bishop shall himself obtain the testimonials. A candidate may have received dimissorial letters from his own bishop to be ordained by the bishop of diocese B. Before his ordination (on the strength of the dimissorials) he lives three months or six months in diocese B. Additional testimonials become necessary. The bishop of diocese B is obliged to obtain them; no other Ordinary is obliged to do so.

The next two canons speak of the recipients of dimissorial letters.

Canon 961

Litterae dimissoriae mitti possunt ab Episcopo proprio, etiam Cardinali Episcopo suburbicario, ad quemlibet Episcopum, communionem cum Sede Apostolica habentem, excepto tantum, citra apostolicum indultum, Episcopo ritus diversi a ritu promovendi.

Canon 962

Quilibet Episcopus, acceptis legitimis dimissoriis, alienum subditum licite ordinat, dummodo ipse de germana litterarum fide dubitare nullatenus possit, salvo praescripto can. 994, § 3.

58 Canon 994, § 1.

The first canon gives the answer to the question: " To whom may the dimissorial letters be addressed? " The dimissorials may be addressed by the proper bishop [59] to any bishop provided he is in communion with the Apostolic See and belongs to the rite of the ordinand. It is not necessary to direct the dimissorial letters to one certain bishop.[60] The direction may read *ad quemcumque episcopum catholicum vel ad quemcumque episcopum gratiam et communionem cum sede apostolica habentem.* It appears very proper that the dimissorial letters be addressed not necessarily to one certain bishop because it is commonly understood that the dimissorial letters are granted in favor of the ordinand, not in favor of the ordaining bishop.[61]

The proper bishop for ordination may, however, address the dimissorials for any of his subjects to a certain bishop mentioning him by name. Reiffenstuel [62] and Schmalzgrueber [63] call such dismissorial letters " special " whereas if they are addressed to any bishop they are called " general ". There existed in the former law the restriction which forbade the Cardinal Bishops of the suburbicarian Sees near Rome to send their subjects to any other bishop except the Cardinal Vicar of Rome if they themselves did not ordain. This law is found in the Constitution of Alexander VII, *Apostolica solicitudo* [64] and the Constitution *Apostolicae Sedis* of Pius IX, October 5, 1869.[65] This restriction is abrogated in the new law. Every proper bishop even the suburbicarian Cardinal bishops can direct dimissorials to any bishop who is in communion with the Holy See and who is not of a rite different from that of the ordinand.

[59] Canon 956.

[60] Cf. Many, *De Sacra Ordinatione*, n. 63; Gasparri, *De Sacra Ordinatione*, n. 878; Wernz, *Jus Decretalium*, II, n. 29; Reiffenstuel, *Jus Canonicum Universum*, I, XI, n. 114.

[61] Many, *De Sacra Ordinatione*, n. 63; Gasparri, *De Sacra Ordinatione*, n. 878; cf. Augustine, *Commentary*, IV, p. 432.

[62] *Jus Canonicum Universum*, I, XI, n. 114.

[63] *Jus Ecclesiasticum*, III, XI, n. 50.

[64] *Bull. R.*, 17, 52-53.

[65] *Bull. Rom.*, 17, 52-53.

"*Communionem cum Sede Apostolica habentem*" excludes a bishop who is a heretic, or a schismatic, or a bishop who is deposed or degraded from the episcopal dignity. It includes all bishops and Ordinaries mentioned in canon 957, also all coadjutor, auxiliary and titular bishops. The question may be asked: Should the proper bishop for ordination grant dimissorial letters to his auxiliary or coadjutor bishop? Mothon [66] states that he should address dismissorials to his auxiliary or coadjutor bishop. It does seem in conformity with the canons that dimissorial letters be issued to these bishops.[67]

In order to confer Orders the recipients of dimissorials must have the necessary power of Orders: this is quite evident from what has been said above. Blat [68] adds that even though the fact (communion with the Holy See) is not expressed in the dismissorials it must be understood to be present in the intention of the bishop who issues the letters. Should a bishop intend otherwise they are not *litterae dimissoriae legitimae.*

The exception concerning the difference of rites is quite clearly added to avoid confusion. A subject of the Latin rite may not be sent to a bishop of an Oriental rite and *vice versa.* A subject of an Oriental rite may not be sent to a bishop of the Latin rite or to a bishop of another Oriental rite. Many [69] refers to particular concessions which were made in individual cases before the Code. The words of the canon, *citra apostolicum indultum* indicate that the legislator may make special concessions in similar cases if he deems such action advisable, e. g. in a country where bishops of the Oriental rite are few in number.

Canon 962 decrees that any bishop may lawfully ordain any subject not his own after he has received legitimate dimissorial letters. There are two special provisions in the canon. The first one is that there be no doubt in his mind about the genuine

[66] *Institutions Canoniques,* II, art. 2049, footnote 9.

[67] Canons 955, 962 and 2373, n. 1.

[68] *Commentarium,* Lib. III, Pars I, n. 308.

[69] *De Sacra Ordinatione,* n. 63; cf. Augustine, *Commentary,* IV, p. 432, footnote 58.

character of the dimissorial letters and secondly that the prescription of canon 994, § 3 be observed. The last provision which concerns itself with additional testimonial letters was treated above.

Quilibet episcopus includes all bishops and Ordinaries referred to in the preceding canon in the words *ad quemlibet episcopum. Legitimis dimissoriis:* the word *legitimis* in connection with *dimissoriae* has occured before in canon 955, § 1. In canon 957, § 2 *litterae dimissoriae* is modified by the phrase *iure requisitas. Legitimis* and *iure requisitas* are synonymous terms in their modification of *litterae dimissoriae.* These terms signify that the requirements of the canonical prescriptions as contained in the canons on dimissorial letters must be fulfilled. If they are carried out then the dimissorials are legitimate. Fortified with such dimissorial letters the bishop may licitly ordain a *subditus alienus.* There is no question of valid ordination here. The bishop may ordain provided he does not doubt the genuineness of the letters. He may assure himself of their genuine character in whatever manner he pleases. Positive arguments that he is certain of their genuineness are not required by the canon. Authenticity of the letters is commonly established beyond any reasonable doubt if the signature and seal of the issuing bishop are attached to the dimissorials.[70] Forgery, however, is not entirely excluded. Canon 2374 mentions forged dimissorial letters.

PENAL SANCTIONS

Canon 2373, n. 1 states that any one who ordains the subject of another without the dimissorial letters of his proper Ordinary shall be suspended from the conferring of Orders for a year. This suspension is incurred *ipso facto* and is reserved to the Holy See.

Canon 2373, n. 2 imposes a suspension *ipso facto* upon the Ordinary who ordains his own candidates without obtaining the testimonials referred to in canons 993, n. 4 and 994. The Ordinary is suspended for one year and his suspension is re-

[70] Augustine, *Commentary,* IV, p. 432.

served to the Holy See. It may be asked whether a bishop or proper Ordinary who is suspended from the conferring of Orders can nevertheless grant dimissorial letters. Commentators generally answer in the affirmative because he is not suspended *a jurisdictione*.[71]

A further sanction pertaining to dimissorials is given in canon 2374. This canon states that one who presents himself *malitiose* for ordination without dimissorial letters or with forged dimissorials is at once suspended from the Order received. He shall be punished with severe penalties.

Canon 2409 determines that the Vicar Capitular is subject to suspension *ipso facto a divinis* if he issues dimissorials in violation of the precept of canon 958, § 1, n. 3. This penalty can be traced in the *Liber Sextus* of Boniface VIII.[72] Koeniger [73] seems to think that the same penalty holds for the violation of paragraph two of canon 958. This cannot be admitted since canon 2409 only mentions number three of canon 958.

Canon 963

Litterae dimissoriae possunt ab ipso concedente vel ab eius successore limitari aut revocari, sed semel concessae non exstinguuntur resoluto iure dantis.

This canon considers special juridical elements which enter into all dimissorial letters. They are based on the act of jurisdiction from which flow the dimissorials. The letters are valid if the one who grants them has jurisdiction. The act of jurisdiction gives to the dimissorial letters their juridical value. Their definite value may be limited. Thus canon 963 states that dimissorial letters may be limited or revoked either by the one who issues them or by his successor in the office.

The first juridical element which may affect the dimissorial letters is limitation.

[71] Gasparri, *De Sacra Ordinatione*, n. 876; Many, *De Sacra Ordinatione*, n. 65.

[72] C. 3, *de temporibus ordinationum et qualitate ordinandorum*, I, 9 in VI.

[73] *Katholisches Kirchenrecht*, p. 143.

1) He who grants the letters may give a time limit stating a time within which the ordination should take place.[74] After that time they are null and void if the ordination has not taken place. If no time limit is given they are valid indefinitely as far as time is concerned.

2) He may limit the letters as to the bishop at whose hands the candidate shall receive Orders.

3) He may restrict the Orders to be received by the candidate.

4) He may express conditions in the dimissorial letters which if not verified shall make the letters null, e. g. if the candidate's health improves, if he passes his examinations. In order to be operative these limitations must be clearly expressed in the letters. They may be placed at the time the letters are granted or after they have been issued and before the ordination has taken place.

The second element which may affect the dimissorials is revocation. It is evident that this revocation of dimissorials must be effected and may be effected before their use. Limitations and revocation may also be brought about by the successor of him who issued them.

The last part of the canon determines that the dimissorial letters remain in force once they have been issued even if the grantor loses his office. It does not matter in what manner he suffers the loss of his office. The reason of this is that they are a favor granted to the ordinand. They are *gratia facta ordinando.* "*Litterae dimissoriae, cum sint quaedam gratia et beneficium, efficaciam habent, et valorem quamdiu non revocantur.*"[75] The *regula juris* number 16 applies here: "*Decet concessum a Principe beneficium esse mansurum.*"[76] Thus, by way of example, a bishop may have granted dimissorial letters but before the candidate is ordained the bishop dies or is transferred. The dimissorial letters remain in force.

[74] Blat, *Commentarium*, Lib. III, Pars I, n. 310.

[75] Schmalzgrueber, *Jus Ecclesiasticum*, III, XI, n. 51; Many, *De Sacra Ordinatione*, n. 65; Reiffenstuel, *Jus Canonicum Universum*, I, XI, n. 139.

[76] *Regulae Juris in VI.*

The words *litterae dimissoriae* in canon 963 are universal in their signification, i. e., they refer also to the dimissorial letters granted in virtue of canon 964.[77] The reason for this statement is quite evident since the prescriptions laid down in this canon for dimissorials may affect the ordination of both the religious and diocesan clergy. They are general norms.

A brief statement of what should be expressed in dimissorial letters may properly summarize and conclude this chapter. Commentators generally find no difficulty in presenting a form which is proper but they do not agree on one definite form.

It has been indicated above that some authors insist on certain matters which must be included in the letters while others advocate their omission. This difference of opinion causes no particular canonical difficulty because all authors are agreed upon the contents and form of the dimissorial letters which are essential.

Among all commentators, former and recent (i. e. before and after the Code) Wernz [78] gives probably the most succinct and adequate definition of dimissorials. An introduction here of his text is considered important. " *Quibus in litteris imprimis accurate exprimenda sunt nomina Praelati dimittentis et Episcopi, ad quem ordinandus dimittitur, nisi quis generaliter ad quemlibet Episcopum catholicum de iure et de facto dimittatur. Praeterea indicandi sunt ordines, ad quos dimissus subditus est promovendus, et praesertim de nomine et cognomine, natalibus, aetate, scientia, moribus, libertate ordinandi ab omni impedimento canonico litteris dimissoriis authenticum testimonium est inserendum.*" Mothon [79] presents a *formulaire dés lettres dimissoriales* in which he combines testimonial letters and dimissorial letters into one letter. He crowds too much into the letter which he calls a dimissorial letter.

The essential content of the dimissorial letters is the authorization given to an ordinand to receive Orders from any

[77] Blat, *Commentarium*, Lib. III, Pars I, n. 310.

[78] *Jus Decretalium*, II, n. 29.

[79] *Institutions Canoniques*, III, p. 296.

bishop other than the candidate's own proper bishop.[80] It has been mentioned above who is the proper bishop and who is to be understood by the term *any bishop*. Accordingly the name of the proper bishop or proper Ordinary who grants authorization should be inscribed in the dimissorial letters, likewise the full name of the candidate (*nomen et cognomen*). If the ordinand is sent to a definite bishop, the name of this bishop should be mentioned otherwise the expression *ad quemcumque vel quemlibet episcopum communionem cum Sede Apostolica habentem* is used. The signature of the grantor should be affixed to the document together with his seal. Further the date must necessarily be given if a time limit is stipulated in the letters. All official documents generally bear the date of their issue. It is quite equally essential that the letters state the Orders to which the candidate may be promoted.[81] A bishop may validly and licitly issue one dimissorial letter for the reception of first tonsure, minor Orders and sacred Orders, e. g., if his candidate is at a great distance and the bishop knows that in the ordinary course of events he will be unable to ordain his subject to any of the Orders. Generally, however, this is not done.

The one who grants the dimissorials may testify to the fitness of the ordinand.[82] Canon 960, § 1 does not demand that the testimony of the candidate's fitness be incorporated in the dimissorial letters.

In summary, then, the content and form of dimissorial letters should be the following:

a) Date of document.
b) Name of grantor.
c) Name of ordinand.
d) General or special designation of bishop who is to ordain the candidate.
e) Mention of Orders to be received by the candidate.
f) Signature and seal of grantor.

[80] Cance, *Le Code de Droit Canonique*, Paris, 1930, Tome Second, p. 376.

[81] Schmalzgrueber, *Jus Ecclesiasticum*, III, XI, n. 50.

[82] Wernz, *Jus Decretalium*, II, n. 29; cf. Raus, *Institutiones Canonicae*, Paris, 1923, p. 91.

CHAPTER THREE

Proper Bishop for the Ordination of Religious

The commentary on canons 964—967 (inclusive) forms the subject matter of this chapter. These canons treat of the ordination of religious and of dimissorial letters for ordinands of religious communities. Former legislation with regard to the ordination of religious was very involved and quite complicated because of the many various privileges and Apostolic Indults granted to religious orders. In the Code many canonical difficulties have been removed. It can be quite safely stated that at no time in the history of ecclesiastical legislation has the ordination of religious been so clearly defined as in the new discipline. This does not mean that all difficulties have been cleared away. Authors still differ because the Code seemingly has not settled the matter to the satisfaction of all canonists. In commenting on the canons pertaining to this subject the difficulties and differences of opinions will present themselves. An adequate solution cannot be given to every problem in regard to the ordination of religious.

Canon 964

Quod attinet ad ordinationem religiosorum:

1. Abbas regularis de regimine, etsi sine territorio *nullius*, potest conferre primam tonsuram et ordines minores, dummodo promovendus sit ipsi subditus vi professionis saltem simplicis, ipse vero sit presbyter et benedictionem abbatialem legitime acceperit. Extra hos fines, ordinatio, ab eodem collata, revocato quolibet contrario privilegio, est irrita, nisi ordinans charactere episcopali polleat;

2. Religiosi exempti a nullo Episcopo ordinari licite possunt sine litteris dimissoriis proprii Superioris maioris;

3. Superiores professis votorum simplicium, de quibus in can. 574, litteras dimissorias concedere possunt dumtaxat ad primam tonsuram et ordines minores;

4. Ordinatio ceterorum omnium alumnorum cuiusvis religionis regitur iure saecularium, revocato quolibet indulto Superioribus concesso dandi professis a votis temporariis litteras dimissorias ad ordines maiores.

The first words of the canon *quod attinet ad ordinationem religiosorum* state the import of the canon. The word *ordinationem* refers to first tonsure, minor Orders and sacred Orders.[1] Upon further examination of this canon and its commentaries it should appear who is the proper bishop for the ordination of religious.

Number one of the canon speaks of the *Abbas regularis de regimine.* He is actual superior of an independent local monastery. He must be an abbot who governs an abbey in his own name independently of every other house of the order. The *Abbot Praeses* of monastic congregations, the Abbot Visitor and the Titular Abbot are excluded.[2] Likewise the Coadjutor Abbot unless his appointment by the Holy See gives him the power. An Abbot *commendatorius*[3] to whom an abbey has been given *in commendam* has no power *jure communi* to ordain because he has no *subditi regulares.* The Abbot *Primas* of the Benedictines has ordinary jurisdiction in the College of St. Anselm. He may confer tonsure and minor Orders on the students of St. Anselm.[4]

1) The Code considers only the abbot *de regimine* even though he be not an abbot *nullius.* Many[5] and other commentators discuss at great length the controversy concerning the validity of ordinations performed by an Abbot and whether

[1] Canon 950.

[2] *Commentarium pro Religiosis,* X (1929), 49 note (20); Many, *De Sacra Ordinatione,* n. 54.

[3] Many, *De Sacra Ordinatione,* n. 57; Wernz, *Jus Decretalium,* II, n. 27; Gasparri, *De Sacra Ordinatione,* n. 942.

[4] *Commentarium pro Religiosis,* X (1929), 49 note (20).

[5] *De Sacra Ordinatione,* n. 54; Gasparri, *De Sacra Ordinatione,* n. 955.

Abbots conferred subdiaconate. It is neither necessary nor helpful to enter into a consideration of the old controversy. There is no particular advantage in re-stating the controversy which obtained previous to the promulgation of the Code because the present canon excludes this controversy.

2) The Abbot *de regimine* must be a priest, *ipse vero sit presbyter.* In the former legislation this requirement was very emphatically stressed.[6]

3) He must have received the abbatial blessing[7] according to the prescription of canon 322 and the *Pontificale Romanum.*[8]

4) Those upon whom the Abbot *de regimine* may validly and licitly confer first tonsure and minor Orders are his own subjects by reason of religious profession.

The four conditions given above must be verified. If any one of them is not fulfilled the ordinations are invalid. If the Abbot is a bishop the ordinations are valid.[9] The Abbot enjoys the delegated power to confer tonsure and minor Orders *ipso jure.*[10] May he exercise this power outside of his own abbey? Canon 964, n. 1 does not restrict his power in this respect. Since the Code does not distinguish it can be concluded that an Abbot may ordain validly anywhere.[11] This statement has more force when compared with canon 957, § 2 where it states that an Abbot *nullius* can confer Orders on his own secular subjects validly only in his own territory but does

[6] C. 1, D. LXIX; c. 11, X, *de aetate et qualitate et ordine praeficiendorum,* I, 14; c. 3, *de privilegiis,* V, 7 in VI; canon 14 of the Second Council of Nice, 787: ... "lectoris autem manuum impositionem licet in proprio monasterio—tantum unicuique monasterii praefecto facere si ipsi praefecto scilicet ab episcopo manus est imposita ad praefecturam hegumni, *dum et ipse presbyter.*"—Mansi 13, 753.

[7] Many, *De Sacra Ordinatione,* n. 51; Wernz, *Jus Decretalium,* II, n. 27; Bouix, *Tractatus de Episcopo,* p. 196.

[8] Pars I, de benedictione abbatis.

[9] Blat refers to the words of the canon, *nisi ordinarius charactere episcopali polleat* and remarks that it is exceptional for an Abbot *de regimine* to be a titular bishop.—*Commentarium,* Lib. III, Pars I, n. 311.

[10] Bouix, *Tractatus de Episcopo,* p. 195.

[11] Canon 11.

not restrict him in regard to the ordination of his own religious subjects.

Number two of canon 964 concerns itself with the granting of dimissorials to exempt religious. The term *religiosi exempti* signifies all members of religious Orders, properly so-called, and all those who by reason of their constitutions make solemn profession.[12] They are exempt *jure communi.*[13] There are certain congregations with only simple vows that also enjoy a papal privilege of exemption.[14] Congregations which are exempt in virtue of papal privilege may be called upon by a bishop who is to ordain their subjects to prove their exemption. If they can produce an official document to that effect or show that the exemption is contained in their approved constitutions they have sufficient proof. Among the exempt religious (*jure communi* or by privilege) are included, for the purpose of ordination, those non-exempt congregations with simple vows or those communities of men without vows which have an indult to issue dimissorial letters to their members. This latter class is included here because of ordination, they are not exempt *jure communi.*

Religiosi exempti may signify then three classes of ordinands, i. e., those who belong 1) to a religious order exempt *jure communi,* 2) to a congregation exempt by special privilege, 3) to a non-exempt congregation or community which has an indult to grant dimissorials. No bishop may licitly ordain any one of them without dimissorial letters from his proper major superior. The ordination would be valid if he did ordain without the proper letters provided the ordaining prelate is a bishop.

Number two of canon 964 does not distinguish between the Orders for which the dimissorial letters may be granted. The

[12] Canons 488, n. 2 and 7, and 615.

[13] Schäfer, *De Religiosis ad Normam Codicis Juris Canonici,* Münster i. W., 1927, n. 51; Pejska, *Jus Canonicum Religiosorum,* 3 ed., Friburgi Brisgoviae, 1927, p. 43; Fanfani, *De Jure Religiosorum,* 2 ed., Taurini-Romae, 1925, p. 370, nn. 351, 352; Jansen, *Ordensrecht,* 2 ed., Paderborn, 1920, pp. 46-47.

[14] E. g. *The Congregation of the Passion* (Passionists).

word *ordinari,* therefore, includes all Orders. Number three of this same canon limits the power of the religious superiors mentioned in number two. The religious superiors can issue dimissorials but only for tonsure and minor Orders to their subjects spoken of in canon 574. The subjects mentioned in canon 574 are men in temporary profession. Three years of temporary vows must precede perpetual profession both in the institutes with simple vows as well as in those who have solemn vows. As long as a subject is only temporarily professed his major superior can grant dimissorial letters only for first tonsure and minor Orders even if the term of temporary profession is longer than three years.

Here a question is to the point. Why is the major superior restricted to first tonsure and minor Orders in the granting of dimissorials to temporarily professed subjects? The first answer is generally that the religious in temporary profession may leave the institute without making perpetual profession. After his temporary vows expire he may not want to take perpetual vows or he may obtain a dispensation from his temporary vows according to canons 638-641 inclusive. Again, according to canon 637 he may not be allowed to take perpetual vows. If then a temporarily professed religious were in major Orders and should leave the institute for any of the above reasons what would become of him?

The Code takes care of a religious in temporary profession who has received sacred Orders either before he entered the order or after he has made temporary profession. Canon 641 states that if a religious in major Orders did not lose his diocese (as determined by canon 585), and returns to the world either at the expiration of his temporary vows or by an indult of secularization, he must go to his own diocese. If he lost his diocese, he cannot exercise his major Orders outside the religious organization until he has found a bishop who is willing to receive him, or until the Holy See has made other provision for him. The Code likewise provides for the temporarily professed religious in major Orders who is dismissed from the institute. Canon 648 says that he is subject to the obligation of those Orders and to the other regulations of Canons 641 and 642. Canon 642 enumerates certain benefices and positions which a secularized cleric is forbidden to hold.

It is only necessary to consider here the case of a temporarily professed religious who has received tonsure or minor Orders and who leaves the institute. Where does he belong? Is he *ipso facto* reduced to the lay state? Must the bishop of the proper diocese which he had in the world receive him? Has the bishop who has ordained him any obligation towards him?

The fact that according to canon 585 a religious automatically loses his proper diocese which he had in the world through perpetual vows (simple or solemn) does not seem to have any special reference to this case. The bishop of the diocese to which the religious belonged in the world does not necessarily have anything to do with the ordination of the religious. The major superior must address, as shall be seen, the dimissorials for his ordination to the bishop of the diocese in which is situated the religious house to which the ordinand belongs. It is this bishop who confers first tonsure on the religious in temporary profession. Upon the reception of tonsure the religious is a cleric. He cannot be a *clericus vagus* for the Code prescribes against such clerics. He must be ascribed to a diocese or to the religious community. It is quite certain that the ordaining bishop does not incardinate this religious into his own diocese. He ascribes him therefore through first tonsure to the religious community of which he is a member and in which he is temporarily professed. This cleric does not belong to the ranks of any diocesan clergy. Even though he has not lost the domicile in his own proper diocese which he had before he entered the religious organization by means of perpetual religious profession this does not mean that a religious temporarily professed who has received first tonsure remains incardinated in that diocese. Ordination and religious profession (perpetual or temporary) are two distinct juridical factors.

Leitner [15] and Schäfer [16] seem to hold that the temporarily professed religious in minor Orders who leaves the institute

[15] *Grundriss des Ordensrechtes,* Vienna, 1930, p. 604, footnote 1.

[16] *De Religiosis,* n. 553.

is reduced to the lay state. They base their claim on canons 648 and 669, § 2. The application of these canons is objected to because reduction to the lay state of a cleric in minor Orders upon dismissal from a religious institute partakes of the nature of a penalty.[17] A cleric who leaves an institute after his temporary vows have expired does not deserve a punishment, therefore, he should not be reduced to the lay state if he wishes to go on to the priesthood. Even though Chelodi [18] does not accept the view of Schäfer and Leitner in so many words he says that the religious in question has the same juridical status as a layman. He does not answer the question how the religious can be incardinated into a diocese if he wishes to be ordained to major Orders after leaving the religious institute. It is clear, of course, that if a religious in temporary profession is dismissed he is *ipso facto* reduced to the lay state.[19] If, however, he received minor Orders before entering into the religious institute he is incardinated into the diocese for whose service he was ordained and belongs to that diocese if he leaves the institute upon the expiration of temporary vows unless he has been excardinated. This still does not definitely answer the question concerning the religious who received minor Orders while temporarily professed and who leaves at the expiration of his temporary profession. Fanfani [20] holds that he is incardinated into the diocese of origin or of domicile according to the canons on domicile. He maintains that it is not unfair to hold a bishop (without whose permission the religious received minor Orders) to grant the cleric admission into his own diocese because the bishop is always free to reduce him to the lay state according to canon 211, § 2. Does the reduction to the lay state by this procedure lose the nature of a penalty? It would seem so. And yet it must be remembered that every reduction to the lay state does not necessarily have the nature

[17] Schaaf, *Episcopus Proprius Ordinationis Religiosorum*, *A. E. R.*, 90 (1934), 495.

[18] *Jus de Personis*, n. 108, footnote 1.

[19] Canon 648.

[20] *De Jure Religiosorum*, n. 516.

of a punishment since according to canon 211, § 1 a cleric in minor Orders may of his own free will return to the lay state.

It has been stated above that a cleric, whether religious or secular, must be ascribed to a religious organization or a diocese. The cleric (temporarily professed religious) in question is ascribed to the institute not to a diocese if he received tonsure while in temporary vows. If he leaves the institute after the expiration of the temporary vows he *ipso facto* loses his ascription to the institute. It seems consistent to say that he returns automatically to the lay state because the Code does not admit *clerici vagi vel acephali*.[21] A Coronata maintains that canon 111, § 1 falls by the way and such clerics are *acephali* for they have no proper bishop.[22] Chelodi holds [23] this same opinion when he says, "professus ad tempus qui in religione exempta tonsuram vel ordines minores recepit, nulli dioecesi est adscriptus quare si religiosus esse desierit videtur fieri *acephalus*."

It can hardly be maintained that such a cleric is incardinated in any diocese by first tonsure even if he has not lost his diocese of domicile with or without origin. Domicile alone with or without origin does not effect the incardination of a cleric. It appears then that a cleric who leaves a religious institute is automatically reduced to the lay state not as a punishment but as a necessary juridical effect of the loss of ascription to the institute.

Number four of canon 964 determines definitely 1) that the ordination of all other members of any religious organization is governed by the laws for the diocesan clergy; 2) that every indult granted to superiors for the granting of dimissorials to their subjects in temporary profession is revoked. Who is meant by the *ceterorum omnium alumnorum cuiusvis religionis?* It signifies all members of religious communities not mentioned above. Augustine [24] includes in this class the nov-

[21] Canon 111, § 1.

[22] *Institutiones Juris Canonici*, Taurini, 1928, n. 179.

[23] *Jus de Personis*, n. 108.

[24] *Commentary*, IV, p. 438.

ices of religious orders as well as of congregations. They cannot be admitted here because of canon 567, § 2 which decrees that novices are not to be promoted to Orders during their novitiate. It is quite accurate to say that all religious of non-exempt congregations are governed by canon 964, n. 4 and therefore are to be ordained *jure saecularium*. Among the exempt religious are numbered (as stated above) not only those who are exempt *jure communi* but also those who enjoy a special privilege or have an indult to grant dimissorials. *Jure communi* all congregations with simple vows, temporary or perpetual, are non-exempt unless by reason of papal privelege or indult they cannot be considered under number four of this canon. Besides the religious communities with simple vows who make temporary or perpetual profession there are societies of men living in common without vows. Many of the canons concerning religious apply to these societies because of the fact that canons 673-681 are applied to them. One of these canons, 678, regulates that as far as the reception of Orders is concerned they are bound by the same laws as the secular clergy unless they have an indult to issue dimissorial letters.

The *jus saecularium ad ordinationem* governs a) non-exempt congregations with perpetual profession, b) non-exempt congregations with temporary profession, c) societies without vows. It must be kept in mind that this treatment of number four of canon 964 excludes any privilege or indult.

a) Non-exempt religious congregations with perpetual profession. Members of these congregations must be ordained according to the rules for the ordination of the diocesan clergy. Their superiors cannot grant dimissorial letters. They can present their subjects to the proper bishop for ordination. Who is the proper bishop of ordination for non-exempt religious in perpetual profession? One would expect that canon 956 gives the full answer to this question. Canon 956, however, in its text makes an exception to its general rule when it refers to the candidates of canon 964, n. 4.

Another canon must be invoked in order to obtain a satisfactory answer to the above question, i. e. canon 585. This canon says that he who takes perpetual vows, simple or solemn, loses his own proper diocese which he had in the world. This elimination gives the ordinand with perpetual profession only one proper bishop for ordination, i. e., the bishop of the diocese where the religious house is situated to which the candidate is attached.[25] The perpetually professed religious has a domicile in the place where he is stationed as a member of the religious family of a certain house.[26] This fact makes the bishop of the diocese where the house is located the proper bishop of ordination for all its members who are to be promoted to Orders. The ordinands need not take the oath to remain in the diocese because they are not incardinated into the diocese of the ordaining bishop but into the religious organization.

Vermeersch [27] and most authors maintain that the force of perpetual profession is to incardinate the professed (not a cleric) into the religious community absolutely and perpetually.[28] Temporary profession makes the ascription of a religious (not a cleric) *inchoativa seu conditionalis.*[29]

The bishop in whose diocese the religious house is located is bound to ordain members of that house when they are presented to him by the superior for Orders. He may refuse to ordain them if he should judge that some of the canonical requirements have not been met.[30] Since he is the proper bishop for ordination he may also grant dimissorial letters for the ordination of these candidates. Should he refuse to ordain the religious or to grant dimissorials for them the religious superiors may have recourse to the Holy See if they judge the refusal unjust.[31]

[25] Canon 965.

[26] *Commentarium pro Religiosis*, II (1921), 304.

[27] *Epitome*, I, n. 684.

[28] Coronata, *Institutiones*, n. 179.

[29] Coronata, *Institutiones*, n. 179.

[30] Canon 997.

[31] Gasparri, *De Sacra Ordinatione*, n. 921; Many, *De Sacra Ordinatione*, n. 161.

The religious superiors may not present their subjects to another bishop for ordination even if the circumstances of canon 966, § 1 obtain because the religious superiors in this case of canon 964, n. 4 do not have the right to issue dimissorials. It would be of no avail to ask a bishop other than the proper diocesan bishop to ordain their subjects without dimissorial letters. The superiors may ask the proper bishop to issue dimissorial letters so that their subjects may be ordained at the hands of another bishop.

There appears to be no special allowance made for the ordination of religious *jure saecularium* by a Vicar Capitular or Administrator within a year after the vacancy of the diocese. They cannot *per se* be placed in the class of *arctati* mentioned above.[32]

b) Non-exempt religious congregations with temporary profession.

There are some non-exempt congregations whose members never make perpetual profession. They renew their temporary vows.[33] To this class may be added (as far as ordination is concerned) the religious of non-exempt congregations who are only in temporary profession preliminary to perpetual profession or whether he be a member of a non-exempt congregation which has only temporary profession. The one question pertains to both. They are both in temporary profession and belong to non-exempt congregations. The question is: who is the proper bishop of ordination for non-exempt religious in temporary profession?

The canon clearly states that they are to be ordained *jure saecularium*. This statement does not remove all difficulties. Some authors [34] hold the opinion that the bishop in whose diocese the religious ordinand had a domicile before he entered religion is the proper bishop for ordination. They invoke canon 585 and base their arguments on the fact that one does

32 Canon 958, § 1, n. 3.

33 Canon 488, n. 1.

34 Cf. Schaaf, *Episcopus Proprius Ordinationis Religiosorum*, *A. E. R.*, 90 (1934), 500.

not lose his proper diocese by temporary profession. Fanfani [35] considers the question but his answer is vague. His answer is especially weakened when he says, "episcopus proprius poterit esse, ut nobis videtur, vel episcopus originis—cum professi temporarii non amittant propriam dioecesim—vel episcopus domicilii aut *quasi-domicilii*." Quasi-domicile has nothing to do with the proper bishop for ordinaton.

Since then a religious in temporary profession does not lose his proper diocese and since the religious under immediate consideration must be ordained *jure saecularium* it seems to follow that the bishop of the diocese where the religious has a domicile with or without origin is his proper bishop for ordination.

In keeping with what has been said in Chapter one of this commentary it seems consistent to hold that a cleric, who has been ascribed to a religious institute by first tonsure, belongs permanently to the institute as far as the reception of Orders is concerned. The fact that he does not lose his proper diocese does not exclude another bishop from becoming the proper bishop of his ordination.

The term *jure saecularium* of canon 964, n. 4 and of canon 982, § 3 does not make the bishop of domicile the only proper bishop for the ordination of religious who are governed by these respective canons. As far as the title of ordination is concerned only those religious are affected who never make perpetual profession.[36] Fanfani [37] in speaking of the title of ordination for religious comments briefly on canon 982, § 3: "*Ceteri religiosi* (canon 964, n. 4) omnes scilicet, qui non habent vota solemnia vel saltem simplicia perpetua." It is true that the bishop must provide every one of the non-exempt religious who only take temporary vows with an ordination title.[38]

It may be asked what is the full import of the term *jure saecularium?*

[35] *De Jure Religiosorum,* n. 285.

[36] Canon 982, § 3.

[37] *De Jure Religiosorum,* n. 284.

[38] Canon 980, § 3; canon 974, n. 7.

1) The religious superiors of those who are to be ordained *jure saecularium* cannot grant dimissorial letters to any of their subjects, whether in temporary or perpetual profession. They may present their subjects for ordination to the proper bishop.

2) The bishop of the diocese in which the religious had a domicile with or without origin before he entered the religious institute is the proper bishop for the conferring of first tonsure, minor Orders and sacred Orders.

3) Canon 980, § 2 states that the bishop must provide a canonical title for the religious whom he ordains *jure saecularium.* This must be a title recognized in the constitutions of the institute.

c) Societies of men without vows.

Societies of men living in common without vows [39] present the last group of candidates who are to be ordained *jure saecularium.* Some of these religious communities have an indult to grant dimissorial letters; if so, then the ordination of their members is governed by the indult, not by the *jus saecularium.* It has been stated above that for the most part the government of these religious societies partakes of the government and rules for religious congregations with vows. Whatever their government might be the Code establishes that candidates for Orders from these institutes must be ordained *jure saecularium* (unless they enjoy a privilege or an indult). What is the application of *jus saecularium* to these ordinands? Canon 678 states that in all matters concerning the reception of Orders the members of the society are bound by the same laws as the diocesan clergy unless special regulations have been made for the society by the Holy See. Commentators [40] on canon 678 generally couch their interpretation of this canon in words similar to this quotation from Schäfer: "Relate ad ordines valent can. 955, 956, 979, 976, 993 ideoque omnino reguntur

[39] E. g. Paulists (C. S. P.), Josephites (C. S. J.), Maryknoll Missionaries (M. M.), Congregation of the Most Precious Blood (C. PP. S.).

[40] Vermeersch-Creusen, *Epitome*, I, n. 777; Fanfani, *De Jure Religiosorum*, n. 526; Schäfer, *De Religiosis*, n. 605.

jure Clericorum saecularium salvis privilegiis apostolicis. Litterae dimissoriae dantur ab Ordinario loci, non a Superioribus Societatis, titulus ordinationis non est titulus paupertatis, vel mensae communis vel Congregationis." [41]

If the laws governing the ordination of diocesan clergy apply in full to the members of these societies there should not be any particular canonical difficulty in finding a proper bishop for their ordination. There is no need of bringing into this discussion the matter of *domicilium necessarium seu legale* [42] in order to ascertain who is the proper bishop for ordination. The canons referred to by Schäfer (in the above quotation) do not speak of a necessary or legal domicile in a house of the society. In following the interpretation of canon 956 given above it appears quite clearly that members of these religious societies without vows are at the reception of tonsure incardinated into the diocese of the bishop who is their proper bishop for tonsure unless the particular society enjoys an indult or a privilege. Any final oath or promise the members may have taken to remain perpetually in the society does not give them ascription to the society in the same manner as does profession, temporary or perpetual. There is a special rule which forbids superiors of these societies to present their members except for tonsure or minor Orders as long as the candidates have not taken the final oath or promise binding them perpetually to the institute. Neither may the superiors grant dimissorials (if they have an indult) until the candidates have taken the oath or promise. In societies without vows—after the making of the perpetual and definite choice—superiors are likewise strictly forbidden to promote their members to sacred Orders before the expiration of three full years from the time of the first reception of the novices into the society.[43]

[41] Schäfer, *De Religiosis*, n. 605.

[42] Goyeneche, S., "Consultationes", *Commentarium pro Religiosis*, I (1920), 178.

[43] S. C. de Rel. Instruction, December 1, 1931, n. 15,—*A. A. S.*, 24 (1932), 74; *A. E. R.*, 86 (1932), 617-618.

The proper bishop of ordination must provide the cleric with an ordination title. If the member of a society without vows leaves the institute he must return to the diocese of his incardination, it matters not where the house is located in which he renders service.[44] This opinion finds confirmation in the solution of the *dubia* given by the Congregation of Bishops and Regulars on May 9, 1864.[45] Another decision of the same Congregation may be cited as bearing witness to the fact that the above opinion is tenable.

I. An et quomodo Episcopus (A) ad sacram Ordinationem admittere possit alumnos Instituti (B) ex fide Superioris domus declarantis, eosdem alumnos adscriptos esse eidem domui; vel potius necessariae sint litterae dimissoriae et testimoniales Episcopi originis, seu domicilii, juxta formam Constitutionis Innocentii XII. quae incipit: *Speculatores.*

II. An et quomodo idem dici debeat, quoad alumnos iam promotos ad tonsuram, vel ad aliquem ordinem.

IV. An in casu egressus ab Instituto per dimissionem, aut dispensationem, iidem alumni subjiciantur jurisdictioni Episcopi dioecesis, in qua sita est domus cui adscripti sunt; vel potius illi Episcopo cui subjecti erant priusquam Instituto adscriberentur.

Ad I. Negative ad primam partem, affirmative ad secundam.

Ad II. Affirmative in omnibus.

Ad IV. Negative ad primam partem, affirmative ad secundam.

The question may occur what then is the distinction[46] between the diocesan clergy and the clerics who are members of

[44] Canon 111, § 1 uses the word *religio.* The societies without vows are not *religiones proprie dictae.* Schäfer says that in the schema of the Code (1912): "Religiones distinguebantur strictu sensu, id est Societates in quibus vota erant perpetua et Religiones, in sensu extensivo, id est Societates in quibus vota ad tempus nuncupantur. Improprie Religiones appelari possunt Societates in tit. XVII, can. 673 ss."—*De Religiosis,* p. 36, footnote 3. It cannot be said that members of societies without vows are incardinated or ascribed by first tonsure to the society.

[45] *A. S. S.*, I, 358-366.

[46] *A. S. S.*, 38, 11-13.

a society without vows? Both belong to the diocese because whereas the members of the societies without vows serve the immediate purpose of the Institute, the latter are, as it were, loaned to the society.

This manner of procedure may cause some inconvenience to the superiors of these institutes because of the various documents that are hereby required for the ordination of every member. Any possible inconvenience has little weight upon the realization of the fact that the bishop must know who is incardinated into his diocese and to whom he must give a canonical title. Bishops may refuse to ordain members of societies without vows or insist that the superiors obtain a papal indult to grant dimissorial letters. The indult generally removes all difficulties. It makes provision for a canonical title. If then the member should leave the society without vows which enjoys an indult he must find a bishop who is willing to receive him.

The phrase *revocato quolibet indulto superioribus concesso dandi professis a votis temporariis litteras dimissorias ad ordines maiores* comes for the most part from the decree *Auctis Admodum* of the Congregation of Bishops and Regulars, November 4, 1892.[47] Every privilege formerly granted to religious superiors in virtue of which they could issue dimissorial letters to their temporarily professed subjects for major Orders has been revoked by the Code. The immediate purpose of this revocation of every indult is to simplify matters with regard to the ordination title. It is to guard against ordinations without title. Should a candidate belong to an institute whose members only take temporary vows his reception of major Orders will depend upon the constitutions of the institute, or upon the obtaining of a canonical title, or upon the indult which the institute may have.

May a religious in temporary vows ever be promoted to major Orders? It may happen that a candidate has finished his course of studies but is kept from sacred Orders until the

[47] *Fontes*, n. 2020.

expiration of his temporary vows. In this case the Holy See may grant an indult permitting the religious to take perpetual vows before the temporary profession expires so that he can be promoted to sacred Orders and still conform to canon 964, n. 3.[48] This shows that the Holy See will rather dispense from the full term of temporary profession than that a religious be promoted to major Orders while in temporary profession.

Canon 965

Episcopus ad quem Superior religiosus litteras dimissorias mittere debet, est Episcopus dioecesis, in qua sita est domus religiosa, ad cuius familiam pertinent ordinandus.

Canon 966

§ 1. Tunc tantum Superior religiosus ad alium Episcopum litteras dimissorias mittere potest, cum Episcopus dioecesanus licentiam dederit, aut sit diversi ritus, aut sit absens, aut non sit ordinationem habiturus proximo legitimo tempore ad normam can. 1006, § 2, vel denique cum dioecesis vacet nec eam regat qui charactere episcopali polleat.

§ 2. Necesse est ut singulis in casibus id Episcopo ordinaturo constet ex authentico Curiae episcopalis testimonio.

Canon 967

Caveant Superiores religiosi ne in fraudem Episcopi dioecesani subditum ordinandum ad aliam religiosam domum mittant, aut concessionem litterarum dimissoriarum de industria in id tempus differant, quo Episcopo vel adbfuturus, vel nullas habiturus sit ordinationes.

The three canons determine the bishop to whom the religious superior must direct the dimissorial letters. It is hardly necessary to remark that the *Superior religiosus* mentioned in these canons must have the power to grant dimissorials in virtue of canon 964. Canon 965 states the general rule. This rule is not absolute, for canon 966 gives exceptions to canon 965. Canon 967 further modifies canon 966.

[48] *Commentarium pro Religiosis,* IV (1923), 146-147.

CANON 965

Episcopus ad quem: This term embraces, 1) the bishop of the diocese, 2) Vicars and Prefects Apostolic,[49] 3) Abbots and Prelates *nullius.*[50] *Superior religiosus* means every superior who has the right to grant dimissorial letters. He must be governed by canon 964 which defines when he has the right to issue dimissorials. One cannot say that only religious superiors exempt *jure communi* are to be understood by the term *superior religiosus* of canon 965 because, as has been seen, some superiors have the right to issue dimissorials in virtue of the privilege of exemption or in virtue of an indult. *Litteras dimissorias mittere debet:* What the content of the dimissorial letters for the ordination of religious should be can be better determined at the close of this chapter. *Episcopus dioecesis* has been defined above. Canon 215, § 2 must be included in this definition. *In qua sita est domus religiosa:* This does not designate any other religious house located in the diocese than the one to which the candidate for Orders belongs, for the canon immediately adds *ad cuius familiam pertinet ordinandus.* Religious superiors may not arbitrarily assign a member to any house solely for the reception of Orders. This is further determined in canon 967.

Canon 965 of the Code is taken almost verbatim from the old law as found in the Constitution,[51] *Impositi Nobis,* of Benedict XIV. It also rests on legislation contained in the Decree of Gratian and in the Decretals.[52]

Gasparri [53] refers to the controversy whether the superior had the right to send his subjects to any Catholic bishop of the same rite or was obliged to direct his subjects to the *episcopus monasterii.* The second opinion prevailed. Pope

[49] In order to be able to confer major Orders these must have episcopal consecration.

[50] Item.

[51] *Fontes,* n. 376.

[52] C. 10, C. XVI, q. 1; c. 3, 1, *de temporibus ordinationum et qualitate ordinandorum,* I, 9 in VI.

[53] *De Sacra Ordinatione,* n. 919.

Clement VIII on March 15, 1596 decreed that the religious superiors must address dimissorials for their subjects *ad episcopum dioecesanum, nempe illius monasterii in cuius familia ab iis ad quos pertinet.* This Clementine decree was incorporated by Benedict XIV in his Constitution, *Impositi Nobis,* February 27, 1747.

Canon 965 presents no particular legal difficulty. It does not exclude the special concession of a privilege to a religious superior whereby he may direct dimissorials to any bishop.[54]

In 1582 the Society of Jesus petitioned the Holy See for the renewal of their privilege to grant dimissorials to any bishop. Pope Gregory XIII made the concession on September 22, 1582 in the Constitution, *Pium et Utile.*[55] Benedict XIV determined that these privileges are not communicable. On July 13, 1886 Leo XIII confirmed the Constitution of Gregory XIII.[56] The Society enjoys this particular right under the present discipline.[57] If any other religious institutes had this right prior to the Code they still have it unless it has been expressly revoked.

CANON 966

This canon gives exceptions to the preceding canon. The religious superior may issue dimissorial letters to a bishop other than the bishop of the diocese mentioned in canon 965, 1) if the diocesan bishop has given permission to that effect, 2) or if he is of a different rite than the ordinand, 3) or if he is absent, 4) or if he does not ordain on the next day prescribed in canon 1006, § 2, 5) or if the diocese is vacant and the one who governs the diocese lacks episcopal consecration. The canon states these five exceptions disjunctively which means that any one of the enumerated reasons is sufficient for the

[54] Vermeersch-Creusen, *Epitome,* II, n. 241.

[55] *Bull. Rom.,* VIII, 397-398.

[56] *A. S. S.,* 19, 49.

[57] Canon 4; Gasparri, *De Sacra Ordinatione,* n. 925; Wernz, *Jus Decretalium,* II, n. 28; Fanfani, *De Jure Religiosorum,* n. 286; canon 2373, n. 4 expresse dicit: *salvo legitimo privilegio.*

religious superior to address the dimissorial letters to another bishop. All five reasons are implied or contained in the old law.[58] The first two are not expressly mentioned in the Constitution, *Impositi Nobis*. Neither did Clement VIII include them in his decree of March 15, 1596 nor Innocent XIII [59] in the confirmation of the Clementine decree. Benedict XIII [60] who took up this same matter in his Constitution made no mention of the first two reasons.

The difference of Rite, as indicated above, always was recognized as a sufficient reason for choosing another bishop unless an Apostolic indult had been granted.[61]

The third and fourth reasons are expressly stated in the old law.[62] In the Code the statement of these reasons is equally clear.

The fifth and last reason is a necessary postulate of the two preceding reasons. This rule is taken from the jurisprudence of the Congregation of the Council.[63] Vacancy must be taken in the strict sense.[64] A *sedes impedita* is not a true vacancy. Neither does the suspension or excommunication of the bishop constitute a vacancy. If the one who governs the diocese has episcopal consecration the religious superior cannot consider the See vacant.

The opening words *tunc tantum* of canon 966 make the enumeration of the five reasons taxative. *Licentiam dederit:* These words signify something new in the Code.[65] *Aut sit absens:* The diocesan bishop cannot be considered absent a)

[58] Benedict XIV, Constitution, *Impositi Nobis*,—*Fontes*, n. 376.

[59] Const., *Apostolici Ministerii*, May 30, 1723,—*Fontes*, n. 280.

[60] Const., *In supremo*, September 23, 1724,—*Fontes*, n. 283.

[61] Benedict XIV, Const., *Etsi Pastoralis*, May 26, 1742,—*Fontes*, n. 328.

[62] Many, *De Sacra Ordinatione*, n. 159; Honorante, *Praxis Secretariae Tribunalis*, cap. XII, note 1; Gasparri, *De Sacra Ordinatione*, n. 922; Wernz, *Jus Decretalium*, n. 28.

[63] Many, *De Sacra Ordinatione*, n. 161; Gasparri, *De Sacra Ordinatione*, n. 922; Wernz, *Jus Decretalium*, II, n. 28.

[64] Augustine, *Commentary*, IV, p. 441.

[65] Blat, *Commentarium*, Lib. III, Pars I, n. 314.

if he has ordinations but refuses to ordain subjects of religious superiors,[66] b) if he confers Orders outside the episcopal city,[67] c) if he is present in the diocese but has another bishop confer Orders in his stead.[68] The bishop of the diocese is considered absent if he is outside the diocese even though another bishop ordains in his place.[69]

Aut non sit ordinationem habiturus proximo legitimo tempore ad normam c. 1006, § 2: A religious superior may send his subjects to a bishop other than the diocesan bishop for ordination if the bishop of the diocese will not confer Orders on the days prescribed in canon 1006, § 2. Some authors [70] hold that the religious superior may address dimissorials to another bishop if the diocesan bishop ordains on the prescribed days but only privately. They demand *general* ordinations. Many [71] on the contrary states that the Clementine decree does not distinguish between general and particular ordinations. He maintains that the religious superior may not direct dimissorial letters *ad quemcumque episcopum* if the bishop ordains privately. He gives this opinion as *saltem probabilius.* Innocent XIII in his Const., *Apostolici ministerii,* May 23, 1723 [72] requires that the ordinations be publicly announced a month before they are to take place. This Constitution of Innocent XIII was at first intended only for Spain, later on Benedict XIV in the Const., *Impositi Nobis,* extended the Constitution of Innocent XIII to the entire world but omitted paragraph 17. It appears that canon 966 does not distinguish between general and particular ordinations. It is mainly concerned with the

66 Gasparri, *De Sacra Ordinatione,* n. 921 and n. 922.

67 Riganti, *Constitutiones et Ordinationes Cancellariae Apostolicae,* cap. 24, n. 255; Many, *De Sacra Ordinatione,* n. 159.

68 Riganti, *Constitutiones et Ordinationes Cancellariae Apostolicae,* cap. 24, n. 256; Gasparri, *De Sacra Ordinatione,* n. 922.

69 Many, *De Sacra Ordinatione,* n. 159; cf. Augustine, *Commentary,* IV, p. 440.

70 Honorante, *Praxis Secretariae Tribunalis,* cap. XII, note 2; Gasparri, *De Sacra Ordinatione,* n. 922.

71 *De Sacra Ordinatione,* n. 158.

72 *Fontes,* n. 280, § 17.

proper time specified in canon 1006, § 2. To bring in this distinction would confuse the legislation since canon 1006, § 2 speaks only of major Orders. Immediately the question occurs what about the conferring of the other Orders? If the bishop of the diocese confers Orders at the *tempus legitimum* even though this conferring of Orders cannot be called general ordination the religious superior cannot allege a reason because of this procedure to send his subjects elsewhere for ordination, since the bishop of the diocese does not exclude them. Even if the socalled particular ordination appears tantamount to a refusal to ordain the subjects of the religious superior still the superior is not free to send his subjects to another bishop.

Ad normam can. 1006, § 2: The words of this paragraph read: "Ordinationes in sacris celebrentur intra Missarum sollemnia sabbatis Quattuor Temporum, sabbato ante dominicam Passionis, et Sabbato Sancto."

Does the reference to canon 1006, § 2 in canon 966, § 1 mean that the law would permit the religious superior to send his subjects to another bishop if the bishop of the diocese does not accede to the special wishes of the superior, e. g., if in virtue of an indult his subjects could be ordained *extra tempora?* The religious superior may not address the dimissorial letters to another bishop if the diocesan bishop refuses to grant him the special favor.[73]

If the bishop does not confer Orders on any one of the six Saturdays but ordains on another day the religious superior may direct his subjects to another bishop. The law grants him this permission even though canon 1006, § 3 says that: "Gravi tamen causa interveniente, Episcopus potest eas habere etiam quolibet die dominico aut festo de praecepto." The text of canon 966, § 1 refers only to canon 1006, § 2.[74]

In the event that a religious superior may address dimissorial letters to any bishop because any one of the five conditions

[73] Many, *De Sacra Ordinatione*, n. 159; Blat, *Commentarium*, Lib. III, Pars I, n. 314.

[74] Cf. Augustine, *Commentary*, IV, p. 441.

obtain he may do so for any Order, from first tonsure to the priesthood inclusive provided he observes the rules of canon 964, nn. 2 and 3.[75]

CANON 966, § 2

Paragraph two demands the authentic statement of the episcopal curia in every case to the effect that one of the five conditions is verified. The demand is couched in the words *necesse est.* Honorante states plainly that this prescription was made in order to avoid fraud.[76]

This document may be issued by the Vicar General, Vicar Capitular or Administrator, Chancellor of the diocese or the Secretary of the bishop of the diocese. It must have their signature and the seal of the diocese.[77] If this document does not accompany the dimissorial letters issued by the religious superior the dimissorial letters are not legitimate and the bishop may not ordain the religious under pain of suspension.[78]

CANON 967

This canon likewise adopts the words of the Constitution, *Impositi Nobis.* It cautions the religious superiors against committing fraud. Fraud is expressly forbidden in this canon. It is not to be presumed and it is quite difficult to prove fraud.[79]

Caveant: Religious superiors are warned against transgressions of the preceding canons. Canon 2410 decrees the penalty for religious superiors who violate the precepts of canons 965-967. They are *ipso facto* suspended for one month from the celebration of Mass. The Pontifical Commission for the Authentic Interpretation of the Code, June 3, 1918, declared that canon 2410 also applies to societies of clerics without vows

[75] Many, *De Sacra Ordinatione*, n. 159.

[76] *Praxis Secretariae Tribunalis*, cap. XII, note 1.

[77] Blat, *Commentarium*, Lib. III, Pars I, n. 314.

[78] Canon 2373, n. 4.

[79] Many, *De Sacra Ordinatione*, n. 159.

if the society has the privilege of granting dimissorial letters to its members.[80]

Superiores religiosi are those mentioned in canon 965. *Ne in fraudem:* The actions of the religious superior are fraudulent if they hide his true intention of avoiding the right of the diocesan bishop to ordain his subjects. Thus, if in order to avoid the bishop of the diocese a religious superior would send his subjects (candidates for Orders) to another religious house, *subditum ordinandum ad aliam religiosam domum mittant.* The superiors may fear that the bishop of the diocese will reject their subjects and because of this they send them to another house temporarily.[81] There is no fraud, however, if they transfer them permanently to another house in another diocese with the knowledge that their ordination will take place with less trouble, or if for some other just cause they make a transfer, e. g., for study, health or vacation.

The canon further states that the religious superior acts *in fraudem legis* if he intentionally delays the issuance of dimissorial letters to a time when the bishop either is absent or will not ordain.

De industria in id tempus differant: It will be difficult to ascertain the intention of the religious superior in this matter whether or not he has committed fraud. It may easily happen that many frauds of this nature remain unknown to men nevertheless they are known to God and the conscience of the religious superior who transgresses the law.

The formula of dimissorial letters for the ordination of exempt religious differs from that for the diocesan clergy. In view of what has gone before in this chapter and in the chapter on dimissorial letters the content and form of dimissorial letters for exempt religious can be given summarily as follows:

a) Date of document.
b) Name of grantor. (Full name and title of major superior.)

[80] *A. A. S.*, 10 (1918), 347.

[81] Blat, *Commentarium*, Lib. III, Pars I, n. 314.

c) Name of ordinand.
d) Designation of the bishop who is to ordain the candidate.
e) Mention of Orders to be received by the candidate.
f) Testimony of the grantor to the fitness of the candidate.
g) Religious profession of candidate, whether temporary or perpetual, whether simple or solemn.
h) Name of the monastery to which the candidate belongs.
i) Statement of exemption, *jure communi,* by privilege, or by indult.
j) Signature of grantor and seal of religious order.

BIBLIOGRAPHY

Sources

Acta Sanctae Sedis, 41 vols., Rome, 1865-1908.

Acta Apostolicae Sedis, Typis Polygottis Vaticanis, 1909-

Acta et Decreta Conciliorum Recentiorum (Collectio Lacensis), 7 vols., Friburgi Brisgoviae, 1870-1890.

Bullarium Romani Continuatio Summorum Pontificum, 19 vols., Prato, 1756-1883.

Bullarium Magnum Romanum, Tomus Primus, Luxemburgi, 1727.

Bullarium Diplomatum et Privilegiorum Sanctorum Romanorum Pontificum, Taurinensis Editio, 24 vols., 1857-1872.

Bullarium Pontificium Sacrae Congregationis de Propaganda Fidei, Tomus Primus, Romae, 1839.

Codex Iuris Canonici, Rome, 1918.

Codicis Iuris Canonici Fontes, cura Emi. Petri Card. Gasparri editi, 6 vols., Rome, 1923-1933.

Concilii Plenarium Baltimorensis, II, Acta et Decreta, Baltimore, 1868.

Concilii Plenarii Baltimorensis, III, Acta et Decreta, Baltimore, 1886.

Concilii Plenarii Americae Latinae, Acta et Decreta, 1900.

Corpus Iuris Canonici (Richter-Friedberg), 2 vols., Leipzig-Welter, 1922.

Corpus Iuris Civilis (Krueger-Mommsen-Schoell-Kroell), 5 ed., 3 vols., Berlin, Weidman, 1928.

Denzinger, H. - Bannwart, C., *Enchiridion Symbolorum*, Editio 18-20, Friburgi Brisgoviae (Herder), 1932.

Harduin, Jean, *Acta Conciliorum et Epistolae Decretales ac Constitutiones Summorum Pontificum*, 12 vols., Parisiis, 1715.

Hartzheim, J., S.J., *Concilia Germaniae*, 11 vols., Coloniae Augustae Agrippinensium, 1759-1790.

Mansi, J., *Sacrorum Conciliorum Nova et Amplissima Collectio*, 53 vols., Paris-Arnheim-Leipzig, 1901-1927.

Migne, J., *Patrologiae Cursus Completus*—Series Latina, 221 vols., (MPL), Paris, 1844-1855; Series Graeca, 161 vols. (MPG), Paris, 1858-1864.

Pontificale Romanum, Mechliniae, 1875.

Richter-Schulte, *Canones et Decreta Concilii Tridentini*, Leipzig, 1853.

Thesaurus Resolutionum Sacrae Congregationis Concilii, 167 vols., Romae, 1718-1908.

Reference Works

Aichner, S., *Compendium Iuris Ecclesiastici, Editio Sexta*, Brixinae, 1887.

Baart, P., *Legal Formulary*, Third Edition, New York, 1898.

[Bachofen], Charles Augustine, *A Commentary on the New Code of Canon Law*, 4 ed., 8 vols., St. Louis (Herder), 1921-1929.

Blat, A., *Commentarium Textus Codicis Canonici*, Romae, 1924.
Bouix, D., *Tractatus de Episcopo*, Tomus Secundus, Parisiis, 1859.
Bouuaert, J. – Simenon, G., *Manuale Iuris Canonici*, Gandae et Leodii, 1931.
Buoncore, Guiseppe, *Il " Titulus Canonicus"*, Napoli, 1933.
Bouscaren, T., *The Canon Law Digest*, Milwaukee (Bruce), 1934.
Cance, A., *Le Code de Droit Canonique*, Tome Second, Paris, 1920.
Chelodi, J., *Jus de Personis, Editio Altera*, Tridenti, 1927.
Coronata, M., O.M.Cap., *Institutiones Iuris Canonici*, Turin, 1928.
Duchesne, L., *Liber Pontificalis*, Vol. I, Paris, 1886.
Du Cange, *Glossarium ad Scriptores Mediae et Infimae Latinitatis*, Tom. II, Parisiis, 1733.
Eichmann, E., *Lehrbuch des Kirchenrechts auf Grund des Codex Iuris Canonici*, 2 ed., Paderborn, 1926.
Fanfani, L., O.P., *De Iure Religiosorum*, 2 ed., Taurini-Romae, 1925.
Ferraris, L., *Prompta Bibliotheca Canonica*, Parisiis, 1865.
Forcellini, *Lexicon Totius Latinitatis*, Editio in Germania, T. IV, Schneebergae, 1835.
Fuchs, V., *Der Ordinationstitel von seiner Entstehung bis auf Innocenz III*, Bonn, 1930.
Gasparri, P., *Tractatus Canonicus de Sacra Ordinatione*, 2 vols., Parisiis, 1894.
Hefele, Carl, *Conciliengeschichte*, 2 ed., 9 vols., Freiburg im Breisgau, 1873-1890.
Hinschius, P., *System des Katholischen Kirchenrechts*, Vol. I, Berlin, 1869.
Honorante, R., *Praxis Secretariae Tribunalis*, Secunda Editio, Romae, 1762.
Jansen, J., O.M.I., *Ordensrecht*, Zweite Auflage, Paderborn, 1920.
Kober, F., *Die Suspension der Kirchendiener*, Tuebingen, 1862.
Koeniger, A., *Katholisches Kirchenrecht*, Freiburg im Breisgau, 1926.
Kurtscheid, B., *Das Neue Kirchenrecht*, 2 ed., Paderborn, 1921.
Leitner, *Grundriss des Ordensrechtes*, Vienna (Auer), 1930.
Lupus, C., *Opera Omnia Canonica*, Tom. IX, Venetiis, 1727.
Many, S., *Praelectiones de Sacra Ordinatione*, Parisiis, 1905.
Mathis, Burkhard, O.M.Cap., *Die Privilegien des Franziskaner-Ordens bis zum Konzil von Vienne (1311)*, Paderborn, 1927.
Mejer, O., *De Titulo Missionis Apud Catholicos*, Regiomanti, 1848.
Michiels, G., O.M.Cap., *Principia Generalia de Personis in Ecclesia*, Lublin, 1932.
Mothon, J., O.P., *Institutions Canoniques*, Vols. II and III, Bruges, 1924.
Neuberger, N. J., *Canon 6 or The Relation of the Codex Iuris Canonici to Preceding Legislation*, Washington, D. C., 1927.
Noldin, *De Sacramentis*, III, Editio XIX, Oeniponte, 1929.
Noval, J., *Codificationis Iuris Canonici Recensio-Historico-Apologetica et Codicis Piano Benedictini Notitia Generalis*, Romae, 1918.
Ojetti, B., S.J., *Commentarium in Codicem Iuris Canonci*, Liber Secundus, Romae, 1930.
Panormitanus, Abbas (Nicolaus de Tudeschis) *Commentaria in quinque Libros Decretalium*, 8 vols., Venice, 1578.

Pejska, J., *Jus Canonicum Religiosorum*, 3 ed., Friburgi Brisgoviae, 1927.

Perathoner, A., *Das Kirchliche Gesetzbuch*, Brixen, 1923.

Pruemmer, D., O.P., *Manuale Iuris Canonici*, Editio Quarta et Quinta, Friburgi Brisgoviae, 1927.

Raus, J. B., *Institutiones Canonicae*, Paris, 1923.

Riganti, J. B., *Constitutiones et Ordinationes Cancellariae Apostolicae*, Tomus I, Colloniae Allobrogum, 1751.

Reiffenstuel, A., *Jus Canonicum Universum*, Vol. I, Parisiis, 1864.

Schäfer, T., O.M.Cap., *De Religiosis ad Normam Codicis Iuris Canonici*, Münster i. W., 1927.

Sebastianelli, G., *Praelectiones Iuris Canonici*, 2 ed., Romae, 1905.

Schmalzgrueber, F., *Jus Ecclesiasticum Universum*, Vol. II, Romae, 1844.

Thomassinus, L., *Vetus et Nova Ecclesiae Disciplina*, Pars II, Liber I, Parisiis, 1688.

Van Espen, Z. B., *Jus Ecclesiasticum Universum*, Vols. I and II, Venetiis, 1769.

Vecchiotti, S., *Institutiones Canonicae*, Editio decimanona, Augustae Taurinorum, 1886.

Vermeersch, A.-Creusen, J., *Epitome Iuris Canonici*, 4 ed., 3 vols., Mechlin, 1930.

Wernz, F. X., *Jus Decretalium*, Tomus Secundus, Romae, 1906.

Woywod, S., O.F.M., *A Practical Commentary on the Code of Canon Law*, 2 vols., New York, 1926.

Periodicals

American Ecclesiastical Review (AER), Philadelphia, 1889-

Apollinaris, Rome, 1928-

Archiv für katholisches Kirchenrecht (AKKR), Mainz, 1857-

Commentarium pro Religiosis, Romae, 1920-

Irish Ecclesiastical Record (IER), Dublin, 1864-

Irish Theological Quarterly, Dublin, 1906-1922.

Il Monitore Ecclesiastico, Rome, 1879-

Jus Pontificium, Rome, 1921-

Le Canoniste Contemporain, Paris, 1878-

Nouvelle Revue Théologique, Paris, 1869-

Periodica de re canonica et morali utili praesertim Religiosis et Missionariis, Bruges, 1905-

Zeitschrift für Katholische Theologie, Innsbruck, 1877-

ALPHABETICAL INDEX

BIOGRAPHICAL NOTE

John M. Moeder was born at Red Wing, Kansas, November 12, 1903. He attended the parochial schools in the diocese of Wichita, Kansas,—St. Mark's, Colwich; St. Joseph's, Ellinwood and St. Joseph's, Liebenthal. At St. Lawrence College, Mt. Calvary, Wisconsin, he completed four years' high school and a two years' college course. His seminary course was made at Kenrick Seminary, Webster Groves, Missouri. On May 30, 1931, he was ordained to the priesthood. In September, 1932, he enrolled in the School of Canon Law at the Catholic University of America, where he received the Baccalaureate and Licentiate in Canon Law.

UNIVERSITAS CATHOLICA AMERICAE

WASHINGTON, D. C.

FACULTAS JURIS CANONICI

1935

No. 95

CANON LAW STUDIES

1. Freriks, Rev. Celestine A., C.PP.S., J.C.D., Religious Congregations in Their External Relations, 121 pp., 1916.
2. Galliher, Rev. Daniel M., O.P., J.C.D., Canonical Elections, 117 pp., 1917.
3. Borkowski, Rev. Aurelius L., O.F.M., De Confraternitatibus Ecclesiasticis, 136 pp., 1918.
4. Castillo, Rev. Cayo, J.C.D., Disertacion Historico-canonica sobre la Potestad del Cabildo en Sede Vacante o Impedida del Vicario Capitular, 99 pp., 1919 (1918).
5. Kubelbeck, Rev. William J., S.T.B., J.C.D., The Sacred Penitentiaria and Its Relations to Faculties of Ordinaries and Priests, 129 pp., 1918.
6. Petrovits, Rev. Joseph J. C., S.T.D., J.C.D., The New Church Law on Matrimony, X-461 pp., 1919.
7. Hickey, Rev. John J., S.T.B., J.C.D., Irregularities and Simple Impediments in the New Code of Canon Law, 100 pp., 1920.
8. Klekotka, Rev. Peter J., S.T.B., J.C.D., Diocesan Consultors, 179 pp., 1920.
9. Wannenmacher, Rev. Francis, J.C.D., The Evidence in Ecclesiastical Procedure Affecting the Marriage Bond, 1920. (Not Printed.)
10. Golden, Rev. Henry Francis, J.C.D., Parochial Benefices in the New Code, IV-119 pp., 1921. (Printed 1925.)
11. Koudelka, Rev. Charles, J., J.C.D., Pastors, Their Rights and Duties According to the New Code of Canon Law, 211 pp., 1921.
12. Melo, Rev. Antonius, O.F.M., J.C.D., De Exemptione Regularium, X-188 pp., 1921.
13. Schaaf, Rev. Valentine Theodore, O.F.M., S.T.B., J.C.D., The Cloister, X-180 pp., 1921.
14. Burke, Rev. Thomas Joseph, S.T.B., J.C.D., Competence in Ecclesiastical Tribunals, IV-117 pp., 1922.
15. Leech, Rev. George Leo, J.C.D., A Comparative Study of the Constitution "Apostolicae Sedis" and the "Codex Juris Canonici," 179 pp., 1922.
16. Motry, Rev. Hubert Louis, S.T.D., J.C.D., Diocesan Faculties According to the Code of Canon Law, II-167 pp., 1922.
17. Murphy, Rev. George Lawrence, J.C.D., Delinquencies and Penalties in the Administration and the Reception of the Sacraments, IV-121 pp., 1923.
18. O'Reilly, Rev. John Anthony, S.T.B., J.C.D., Ecclesiastical Sepulture in the New Code of Canon Law, II-129 pp., 1923.

19. Michalicka, Rev. Wenceslas Cyrill, O.S.B., J.C.D., Judicial Procedure in Dismissal of Clerical Exempt Religious, 107 pp., 1923.
20. Dargin, Rev. Edward Vincent, S.T.B., J.C.D., Reserved Cases According to the Code of Canon Law, IV-103 pp., 1924.
21. Godfrey, Rev. John A., S.T.B., J.C.D., The Right of Patronage According to the Code of Canon Law, 153 pp., 1924.
22. Hagedorn, Rev. Francis Edward, J.C.D., General Legislation on Indulgences, II-154 pp., 1924.
23. King, Rev. James Ignatius, J.C.D., The Administration of the Sacraments to Dying Non-Catholics, V-141 pp., 1924.
24. Winslow, Rev. Francis Joseph, A.F.M., J.C.D., Vicars and Prefects Apostolic, IV-149 pp., 1924.
25. Correa, Rev. Jose Servelion, S.T.L., J.C.D., La Potestad Legislativa de la Iglesia Católica, IV-127 pp., 1925.
26. Dugan, Rev. Henry Francis, M.A., J.C.D., The Judiciary Department of the Diocesan Curia, 87 pp., 1925.
27. Keller, Rev. Charles Frederick, S.T.B., J.C.D., Mass Stipends, 167 pp., 1925.
28. Paschang, Rev. John Linus, J.C.D., The Sacramentals According to the Code of Canon Law, 129 pp., 1925.
29. Piontek, Rev. Cyrillus, O.F.M., S.T.B., J.C.D., De Indulto Exclaustrationis necnon Saecularizationis, XIII-289 pp., 1925.
30. Kearney, Rev. Richard Joseph, S.T.B., J.C.D., Sponsors at Baptism According to the Code of Canon Law, IV-127 pp., 1925.
31. Bartlett, Rev. Chester Joseph, A.M., LL.B., J.C.D., The Tenure of Parochial Property in the United States of America, V-108 pp., 1926.
32. Kilker, Rev. Adrian Jerome, J.C.D., Extreme Unction, V-425 pp., 1926.
33. McCormick, Rev. Robert Emmett, J.C.D., Confessors of Religious, VIII-266 pp., 1926.
34. Miller, Rev. Newton Thomas, J.C.D., Founded Masses According to the Code of Canon Law, VII-93 pp., 1926.
35. Roelker, Rev. Edward G., S.T.D., J.C.D., Principles of Privilege According to the Code of Canon Law, XI-166 pp., 1926.
36. Bakalarczyk, Rev. Richardus, M.I.C., J.U.D., De Novitiatu, VIII-208 pp., 1927.
37. Pizzuti, Rev. Lawrence, O.F.M., J.U.L., De Parochis Religiosis, 1927. (Not Printed.)
38. Bliley, Rev. Nicholas Martin, O.S.B., J.C.D., Altars According to the Code of Canon Law, XIX-132 pp., 1927.
39. Brown, Brendan Francis, A.B., LL.M., J.U.D., The Canonical Juristic Personality with Special Reference to its Status in the United States of America, V-212 pp., 1927.
40. Cavanaugh, Rev. William Thomas, C.P., J.U.D., The Reservation of the Blessed Sacrament, VIII-101 pp., 1927.
41. Doheny, Rev. William J., C.S.C., A.B., J.U.D., Church Property: Modes of Acquisition, X-118 pp., 1927.

42. Feldhaus, Rev. Aloysius H., C.PP.S., J.C.D., Oratories, IX-141 pp., 1927.
43. Kelly, Rev. James Patrick, A.B., J.C.D., The Jurisdiction of the Simple Confessor, X-208 pp., 1927.
44. Neuberger, Rev. Nicholas J., J.C.D., Canon 6 or the Relation of the Codex Juris Canonici to the Preceding Legislation, V-95 pp., 1927.
45. O'Keeffe, Rev. Gerald Michael, J.C.D., Matrimonial Dispensations, Powers of Bishops, Priests, and Confessors, VIII-232 pp., 1927.
46. Quigley, Rev. Joseph, A.M., A.B., J.C.D., Condemned Societies, 139 pp., 1927.
47. Zaplotnik, Rev. Ioannes Leo, J.C.D., De Vicariis Foraneis, X-142 pp., 1927.
48. Duskie, Rev. John Aloysius, A.B., J.C.D., The Canonical Status of the Orientals in the United States, VIII-196 pp., 1928.
49. Hyland, Rev. Francis Edward, J.C.D., Excommunication, Its Nature, Historical Development and Effects, VIII-181 pp., 1928.
50. Reinmann, Rev. Gerald Joseph, O.M.C., J.C.D., The Third Order Secular of Saint Francis, 201 pp., 1928.
51. Schenk, Rev. Francis J., J.C.D., The Matrimonial Impediments of Mixed Religion and Disparity of Cult, XVI-318 pp., 1929.
52. Coady, Rev. John Joseph, S.T.D., J.U.D., A.M., The Appointment of Pastors, VIII-150 pp., 1929.
53. Kay, Rev. Thomas Henry, J.C.D., Competence in Matrimonial Procedure, VIII-164 pp., 1929.
54. Turner, Rev. Sidney Joseph, C.P., J.U.D., The Vow of Poverty, XLIX-217 pp., 1929.
55. Kearney, Rev. Raymond A., A.B., S.T.D., J.C.D., The Principles of Delegation, VII-149 pp., 1929.
56. Conran, Rev. Edward James, A.B., J.C.D., The Interdict, V-163 pp., 1930.
57. O'Neil, Rev. William H., J.C.D., Papal Rescripts of Favor, VII-218 pp., 1930.
58. Bastnagel, Rev. Clement Vincent, J.U.D., The Appointment of Parochial Adjutants and Assistants, XV-257 pp., 1930.
59. Ferry, Rev. William A., A.B., J.C.D., Stole Fees, X-107 pp., 1930.
60. Costello, Rev. John Michael, A.B., J.C.D., Domicile and Quasi-Domicile, VII-201 pp., 1930.
61. Kremer, Rev. Michael Nicholas, A.B., S.T.B., J.C.D., Church Support in the United States, VI-136 pp., 1930.
62. Angulo, Rev. Luis, C.M., J.C.D., Legislación de la Iglesia sobre la intención en la applicación de la Santa Misa, VII-104 pp., 1931.
63. Frey, Rev. Wolfgang Norbert, O.S.B., A.B., J.C.D., The Act of Religious Profession, VIII-174 pp., 1931.
64. Roberts, Rev. James Brendan, A.B., J.C.D., The Banns of Marriage, XIV-140 pp., 1931.
65. Ryder, Rev. Raymond Aloysius, A.B., J.C.D., Simony, IX-151 pp., 1931.

66. CAMPAGNA, REV. ANGELO, PH.D., J.U.D., Il Vicario Generale del Vescovo, VII-205 pp., 1931.
67. COX, REV. JOSEPH GODFREY, A.B., J.C.D., The Administration of Seminaries, VI-124 pp., 1931.
68. GREGORY, REV. DONALD J., J.U.D., The Pauline Privilege, XV-165 pp., 1931.
60. DONOHUE, REV. JOHN F., J.C.D., The Impediment of Crime, VIII-110 pp., 1931.
70. DOOLEY, REV. EUGENE A., O.M.I., J.C.D., Church Law on Sacred Relics, IX-143 pp., 1931.
71. ORTH, REV. CLEMENT RAYMOND, O.M.C., J.C.D., The Approbation of Religious Institutes, 171 pp., 1931.
72. PERNICONE, REV. JOSEPH M., A.B., J.C.D., The Ecclesiastical Prohibition of Books, XII-267 pp., 1932.
73. CLINTON, REV. CONNELL, A.B., J.C.D., The Paschal Precept, IX-108 pp., 1932.
74. DONELLY, REV. FRANCIS B., A.M., S.T.L., J.C.D., The Diocesan Synod, VIII-125 pp., 1932.
75. TORRENTE, REV. CAMILO, C.M.F., J.C.D., Las Processiones Sagradas, V-145 pp., 1932.
76. MURPHY, REV. EDWIN J., C.PP.S., J.C.D., Suspension Ex Informata Conscientia, XI-122 pp., 1932.
77. MACKENZIE, REV. ERIC F., A.M., S.T.L., J.C.D., The Delict of Heresy in its Commission, Penalization, Absolution, VII-124 pp., 1932.
78. LYONS, REV. AVITUS E., S.T.B., J.C.D., The Collegiate Tribunal of First Instance, XI-147 pp., 1932.
79. CONNOLLY, REV. THOMAS A., J.C.D., Appeals, XI-195 pp., 1932.
80. SANGMEISTER, REV. JOSEPH V., A.B., J.C.D., Force and Fear as Precluding Matrimonial Consent, V-211 pp., 1932.
81. JAEGER, REV. LEO A., A.B., J.C.D., The Administration of Vacant and Quasi-Vacant Episcopal Sees in the United States, IX-229 pp. 1932.
82. RIMLINGER, REV. HERBERT T., J.C.D., Error Invalidating Matrimonial Consent, VII-79 pp., 1932.
83. BARRETT, REV. JOHN D. M., S.S., J.C.D., Comparative Study of the Third Plenary Council and the Code, IX-221 pp., 1932.
84. CARBERRY, REV. JOHN J., PH.D., S.T.D., J.C.L., The Juridical Form of Marriage, 1934.
85. DOLAN, REV. JOHN L., A.B., J.C.L., The Defensor Vinculi, 1934.
86. HANNAN, REV. JEROME D., A.M., S.T.D., LL.B., J.C.L., The Canon Law of Wills, 1934.
87. LEMIEUX, REV. DELISLE A., A.M., J.C.L., The Sentence in Ecclesiastical Procedure, 1934.
88. O'ROURKE, REV. JAMES J., A.B., J.C.L., Parish Registers, 1934.
89. TIMLIN, REV. BARTHOLOMEW, O.F.M., A.M., J.C.L., Conditional Matrimonial Consent, 1934.
90. WAHL, REV. FRANCIS X., A.B., J.C.L., The Matrimonial Impediments of Consanguinity and Affinity, 1934.

91. WHITE, REV. ROBERT J., A.B., LL.B., S.T.B., J.C.L., Canonical Ante-Nuptial Promises and the Civil Law, 1934.
92. REV. ANTHONY PARRA HERRERA, O.C.D., J.C.L., Legislacion Ecclesiastica sobre el Ayuno y la Abstinencia.
93. REV. EDWIN J. KENNEDY, J.C.L., The Special Matrimonial Process In Cases of Evident Nullity.
94. REV. JOHN J. MANNING, A.B., J.C.L., Presumption of Law in Matrimonial Procedure.
95. REV. JOHN M. MOEDER, J.C.L., The Proper Bishop for Ordination and Dimissorial Letters.
96. REV. WILLIAM A. O'MARA, A.B., J.C.L., Canonical Causes for Matrimonial Dispensations.
97. REV. PETER REILLY, J.C.L., Residence of Pastors.
98. REV. MARINER T. SMITH, O.P., S.T.LR., J.C.L., The Penal Law for Religious.
99. REV. DONALD WHALEN, Ph.B., A.M., J.C.L., The Value of Testimonial Evidence in Matrimonial Procedure.

www.ingramcontent.com/pod-product-compliance
Lightning Source LLC
La Vergne TN
LVHW050210080826
844660LV00012B/389

* 9 7 8 0 8 1 3 2 2 2 8 4 4 *